Justice in Middlesex

A BRIEF HISTORY OF THE UXBRIDGE MAGISTRATES' COURT

Justice in Middlesex

A Brief History of the Uxbridge Magistrates' Court

Published by
WATERSIDE PRESS
Domum Road
Winchester SO23 9NN
United Kingdom

Telephone 01962 855567 UK Landline low-cost calls 0845 2300 733
E-mail enquiries@watersidepress.co.uk
Online catalogue and bookstore www.WatersidePress.co.uk

Illustrations Copyright information is listed on p.viii.

ISBN 978 1 904380 399.

Cataloguing-In-Publication Data A catalogue record for this book can be obtained from the British Library.

Cover design © 2007 Waterside Press.

North American distributor International Specialised Book Services (ISBS), 920 NE 58th Ave, Suite 300, Portland, Oregon, 97213-3786, USA Telephone 1 800 944 6190 Fax 1 503 280 8832 orders@isbs.com www.isbs.com

Justice in Middlesex

A BRIEF HISTORY OF THE UXBRIDGE MAGISTRATES' COURT

Eileen M Bowlt

WATERSIDE PRESS

Acknowledgements

This history of the Uxbridge Magistrates' Court and its justices has been told from the point of view of the magistrates. Justices on the Supplemental List who have formed a luncheon club all speak with fondness of their days at Uxbridge court and reflect on the happy atmosphere on the bench there. Many of them have searched their memories and, in some cases, their lofts to provide material for this short history. I should like to thank in particular, Derek Blackwell, Margaret Bunford, Tom Morgan, Paddy Owens, Eric Wise and Joan Woodman. At court, I should like to acknowledge the help of Veronica Clifford and John Milward and the encouragement given by the Centenary Committee. The staff at the London Metropolitan Archives and the members of the Heritage Team at Uxbridge Library have been unfailingly helpful and generous with their time. Fellow local historians Ken Pearce (Uxbridge Record Society) and Philip Sherwood (Hayes and Harlington Local History Society) have exchanged information with me and lent photographs. Above all I thank my husband, Colin, who has always encouraged my interest in local history, supported my endeavours and given practical help in technological matters.

Eileen M Bowlt

September 2007

Justice in Middlesex

CONTENTS

CHAPTER

About the author

Eileen M Bowlt was born and brought up in Yorkshire, but has lived in Middlesex for more than 40 years. A graduate in history and a qualified teacher she has specialised in research on the local history of parishes in north-west Middlesex, resulting in a number of publications: *The Goodliest Place in Middlesex* (1989) (which won the Alan Ball Author Award for Local History); *Ruislip Past* (1994); *Ickenham and Harefield Past* (1996); *Stanmore Past* (1998); *Harrow Past* (2000); and *Around Ruislip* (2007). She has written many articles for local history journals as well as contributing to and advising on other publications.

The author is chairman of the London and Middlesex Archaeological Society, the premier society for people who are interested in London's archaeology, local history and historic buildings, and also of the Ruislip, Northwood and Eastcote Local History Society.

Eileen Bowlt has been a tutor for the Workers' Educational Association, the University of London Centre for Extra-Mural Studies and Birkbeck College Faculty of Continuing Education for more than 30 years. She now teaches courses on the history of London and gives talks to local organizations of all kinds. She was a justice of the peace on the Uxbridge bench from 1989 until transferring to the Supplemental List in May 2007.

She is married to a semi-retired university lecturer and they have four grown-up children and seven grandchildren.

Introduction

There are few books in which the history of a local magistrates' court is recorded for posterity. This book is also unusual in focusing on an area of the country that is rich in legal history and central to developments in the English legal system. Historic connections between Middlesex (which now technically no longer exists), London and Westminster mean that any account of the county and its magistrates must inevitably contain references to well-known places and events: Old Bailey, Newgate, Coldbath Fields, Hicks's Hall, Ludgate, the first stirrings of the Metropolitan Police, Tothill Fields, Tyburn, the Gordon Riots, the Clerkenwell explosion and Middlesex Guildhall to mention just a few.

The Guildhall in Parliament Square, to which justices from Uxbridge and other parts of Middlesex travelled to sit at Quarter Sessions and later the Crown Court, was also the centre of all administration in this part of what is now Greater London. It is scheduled to become the home of the UK Supreme Court from 2009 onwards. Summary justice in these parts has always operated against a fertile backdrop of interest and sometimes intrigue.

I have tried to describe justice both ancient and modern: from the days of draconian punishments for relatively minor offences to more enlightened times and, nowadays, human rights. I have quoted from the records of court proceedings or documents, e.g. about transportation, bridewells, houses of correction, workhouses, and reports of intriguing and illustrative cases. The book also documents – or contains 'snapshots' – of the lives of many individual magistrates, officials, miscreants and pressing issues of the times. Striking are those passages that show how often wealth, power, influence and membership of the bench went hand-in-hand until the determined efforts of later times broadened the composition of the bench and made it more representative of the community that it serves. I should like to think that integrity has remained a constant although there is a reference to at least one instance of what can be styled corruption.

Ultimately, the central focus is on my own bench, Uxbridge, which celebrates the one hundredth anniversary of its courthouse on the day that this book is to be published. Just one of many achievements, I hope that you may agree after reading what follows.

Illustrations

© All other images copyright of the author

CHAPTER 1

Early Justice in an Ancient County

The courthouse at the junction of Harefield Road and Uxbridge High Street was opened on 30 September 1907 by Sir Ralph Littler, who congratulated the local justices on having at last got 'a suitable home for the administration of justice'. For centuries justice in the county of Middlesex (and elsewhere in England and Wales) had been dispensed in public houses smelling of tobacco smoke and spirits, if nothing worse, places that failed to uphold the dignity of the law. In Uxbridge, the justices had used the King's Arms on the High Street probably from the early eighteenth century. In those days it was a busy coaching inn. The very fine timber-framed building still stands today, next door but one to the library and it is now used as offices. In Victorian times court sittings were moved to a more salubrious location, the Public Rooms (later known as the Town Hall) that had been built on the corner of Vine Street and the High Street in 1837. There they remained until 1907.

The frontage of the King's Arms today

The new courthouse was the result of great administrative changes that had taken place since the passing of the Local Government Act 1888, which had set up county councils that took over most of the remaining civic duties formerly performed by justices of the peace. Middlesex, already an oddity because the City of London and the Liberty of Westminster lay within its boundaries, was greatly diminished in size by the establishing of the entirely new county of London, which was carved out of Middlesex and Surrey. Let us look at the ancient county of Middlesex and at what happened in earlier centuries.

Ralph Hawtrey   Eastcote House

Justices of the peace

In 1361, Edward III issued a statute commissioning certain men in each county to keep the peace. In 1362 they were enjoined to hold Sessions of the Peace four times each year to deal with every offence less than a felony (a grave crime). A further enactment of 1414-15 ordered that these sessions should be held in the weeks after Michaelmas (September 29), the feast of the Epiphany (January 6), Easter and the Feast of the Translation of St Thomas Becket (July 7). St Thomas Becket was popular in England in medieval times, especially in London where he was born. Felons were dealt with by the King's justices (senior judges) who travelled the country and held Assizes in the King's name. There were no Assizes in London and Middlesex, but a Commission of Gaol Delivery instead.

Justices of the peace (JPs) were usually landowners or wealthy merchants who were obliged to live in and to own freehold property to a given value within their commission area. The clerk of the peace kept a roll on which justices' names were inscribed after they had been sworn to office. Although respected, perhaps feared, and well-known within the community, JPs were not required to be learned in the law, but since many landowners from the fifteenth century onwards sent their sons to the Inns of Court to give them some polish and help them to understand the management of estates, as well as to Oxford or Cambridge, most justices were well educated. The Hawtreys and their descendants, Rogers and Deanes, who lived at Eastcote House from the sixteenth century and served as local justices, followed this path, as did Robert Ashby of Breakspears in Harefield and many others.

In addition to dealing with breakers of the peace, JPs had manifold administrative duties heaped upon them over the centuries, which included regulating wages under the Statute of Labourers (1388), the supervision of inns (1495 and later licensing provisions), setting rates for the repair and upkeep of bridges (1530) and the maintenance of roads (1550). They dealt with people who failed to attend divine service under Recusancy Acts (1581), organized the relief of disabled soldiers (1592) and set local rates for the relief of the poor as a result of the development of legislation culminating in the great Elizabethan Poor Law of 1601. In the later seventeenth and eighteenth centuries they ordered the removal of paupers to their place of settlement and made bastardy orders whereby fathers had to maintain their illegitimate children. During the eighteenth century local justices of the peace were given greater powers to regulate conditions in prisons (but were reluctant to visit them because of the fear of contracting gaol fever or other life-threatening diseases). JPs became responsible for reformatory schools in 1866 and eventually, in 1883, for lunatic asylums. Such administrative matters were discussed at general sessions held on the days preceding the Quarter Sessions and JPs could claim a subsistence allowance for attending these non-judicial proceedings.

Between sessions, justices acted individually, usually dealing with offenders who had transgressed in minor matters, brought before them by the local constable at home. They took the recognisances (bonds) of the various persons who had to appear at Sessions of the Peace: accused persons, prosecutors, witness who would need to give evidence and people ordered to keep the peace and be of good behaviour.

In those times, villages often had stocks, sometimes a pillory and a cage or lock-up where offenders could be lodged overnight. References to local lock-ups are rather late and, in the absence of such a facility, local alehouses were sometimes used as prisons. The Harefield constable in 1840 kept two gypsies who had seriously assaulted a young man earlier in the evening, at the White Horse in Church Hill, before bringing them before the magistrates the next day. A lock-up was erected behind the new market house in Uxbridge in 1788. Ickenham had one near the church gate, which was apparently used by the Ruislip constable as well, for in 1831 the Ruislip Vestry agreed to build a 'cage for to lodge prisoners in (it being ill-convenient for the constable to take them to Ickenham and elsewhere)'.[1]

Constables were unpaid local officials, who were sworn to office and served for one year. They dealt with any law-breakers in the first instance and had a right to expect assistance from members of the public, who were sometimes reluctant to intervene. The job was onerous, could be dangerous and was not a particularly popular one. From medieval times the constables were elected at the manor court and took their oaths before a local justice.

When the two Ruislip constables, James Seamore and James Atley, had completed their year of office in 1693, they had to apply to the justices to be discharged because the lord of the manor had not held a court leet (a manor court dealing with matters of public jurisdiction) during that time.[2] Later the vestry (the unit of local government that usually met in the vestry of the parish church), nominated constables and the justices confirmed them in office.

Being 'set in the stocks' seems to have been a regular punishment for those who hindered the constables in any way. Robert Batte of Hillingdon, described as a yeoman, in 1609 was ordered to be 'set in the Stocks at Hillingdon the next Market Daie kept at Woxbridge, by the space of three hours, vizt from xi to ii for his contempt in refusing to ayde the Constables apprehendinge a number of Rogues in a Barne at Hillingdon'.[3] In 1617 Richard Godson, a Ruislip joiner, who had abused the constable, John Cogges, in the execution of his office, was first brought before Ralph Hawtrey who took a recognizance from two other Ruislip men to ensure that Godson would answer the charge. He was then ordered 'to be sett in the stocks at Ruislippe before the alehouse dore where he was drunke and did the abuse, to sit there from the beginning of morning prayer until thend [sic] of evening prayer upon Sunday and thence to be brought to the

[1] LMA: DRO19/C1/6.
[2] Middlesex County Records: Session Books 1689-1709, p.89.
[3] Middlesex County Records, Vol II, p.52.

next justices, and in the meantime respited for sureties to be of good behaviour.'[4]

The stocks were also used for the exposure and shaming of offenders. In 1633 Henry Jones, an Uxbridge labourer, pleaded guilty to having a counterfeit passport that certified that the bearer had recently landed at Margate in the Isle of Thanet and was licensed to travel to Minehead in Somerset, recommending him to the charitable consideration of anyone perusing the document. He was ordered 'to be sett upon the pillory one hower in Uxbridge upon a market day with a paper upon his head shewing his offence.'[5]

The stocks in front of Hillingdon Parish Church. From an old print.

Middlesex

Middlesex differed from other counties, being small but populous, including within its boundaries the City of London, the Liberty of Westminster (originally the area over which the Abbot of Westminster had jurisdiction) and the suburban areas around the City, such as Clerkenwell, Holborn and The Strand, as well as the rural parishes. At the beginning of James I's reign in 1603 the population of the built-up metropolitan area is estimated to have been 200,000 and to have grown to 600,000 by 1700. Figures for the entire county are not available until 1801 when the first

---

[4] LMA: SR561/123 in National Register of Archives in conjunction with RNUDC, Catalogue of Exhibition 14-18 July 1953.
[5] Middlesex County Records, Vol III, p.48.

decennial census was taken. There were then about 900,000 people in the county. Burials were continuously more numerous than baptisms in London until the late eighteenth century, so the increase was mainly due to immigration from other parts of the British Isles and abroad.

From medieval times, there was a constant passage of travellers through the county: merchants and tradesmen with business in the City and also people attending the courts of King's Bench and Common Pleas held at Westminster Hall, and sessions of Parliament. The varied throng included bishops, abbots and great lords each with his retinue. Poor people from distant places looking for work, beggars, vagabonds and petty criminals were all attracted by the rich pickings to be found in such a conspicuously wealthy place. Consequently there was more crime than elsewhere and Sessions of the Peace and Gaol Delivery had to be held several times a year.

This pressure of business meant that the freeholders of Middlesex, whether acting as justices, jurors or witnesses at the various courts, were more heavily burdened than in many other counties. There was much overlapping of officials between the City, the county and the Liberty of Westminster. Middlesex freeholders were often citizens of London and many of them lived in Westminster, which comprised the old parishes of St Margaret's, Westminster, and St Martin-in-the-Fields, covering The Strand and much of what is now the West End. In the City the two sheriffs who were elected annually represented the King in London and Middlesex and were responsible for law and order. The sheriffs held their own courts, had their own prisons, the counters, and were responsible for the prisoners in the City's gaols: Newgate Prison (where felons awaited Sessions of Gaol Delivery) and Ludgate Prison (originally for London citizens, mainly debtors). From 1322 there was an under sheriff specifically appointed for the county. During the fifteenth century each sheriff had a more or less permanent under-sheriff and three or four clerks to give legal advice.

The Mayor of London (known as Lord Mayor from the sixteenth century) who presided over his own court, was assisted in legal matters from the fourteenth century by the Common Sergeant and the Recorder. Several recorders progressed to become royal judges. From 1327 the mayor sat with the royal judges when they came into the City. In 1454 Henry VI gave permission for prisoners taken in Middlesex to appear at the Newgate Sessions of Gaol Delivery, rather than at a separate Middlesex

Sessions, although the City and Middlesex prisoners were recorded in different court rolls.

Uxbridge.—High Street.

Uxbridge High Street (c.1920) showing the Assembly Rooms/Town Hall on the left.

The King's Arms Yard: Where courts were once held in a back room

The open-air Justice Hall at Old Bailey

CHAPTER 2

The Middlesex Sessions

Records of the Middlesex Sessions of the Peace survive from 1549. At that date Sessions of the Peace were held at the Castle Tavern in St John's Street, Clerkenwell, just outside the City. A short distance away on the other side of Smithfield, the Commission of Gaol Delivery met in the Justice Hall at Old Bailey beside Newgate within the City.

James I granted the Middlesex justices a piece of land at the bottom of St John's Street in 1609 and one of the justices, Sir Baptist Hicks (later First Viscount Campden), a member of the Mercer's Company and financial agent to the King, paid for a new sessions house to be built on it. The sessions house was ready at the end of 1612 and the first session was held there on 12 January 1613. The 22 justices assembled, having been feasted by Sir Baptist Hicks, decided that it should from henceforth be known as Hicks's Hall. The new building, which looks decent enough from surviving

Hicks's Hall (c.1830)

drawings, displeased some of the inhabitants of St John's Street. Grace Watson, wife of Peter Watson, an apothecary, had to appear 'for giving reviling speeches against Sir Baptist Hicks, touching the building of the

Sessions House' and for her 'unruly behaviour in open court'.[1] Whether she disliked the architecture or the building blocked her view, is not known. A writer in *The Gentleman's Magazine* in November 1827, by which time Hicks's Hall had been long demolished, remembered it as 'a shapeless brick lump, containing a great warehouse in the centre for the court, and houses for the officers all round and joined onto it'. Surviving plans show that the court was oval in shape and a room beneath it was used for dissecting prisoners' corpses publicly in the eighteenth century. Such a scene is depicted in Hogarth's series, *Progress of Cruelty*.[2]

By 1613, Sessions of the Peace were being held eight times a year. They were followed later on the same day or the next with a Commission of Oyer and Terminer to inquire into treasons, rebellions, coining and similar serious felonies. The Commission of Gaol Delivery came a few days later. Lists of justices for the years 1614-1616 have 75 names, presumably the full complement for Middlesex. The names of some of the justices present at quarter sessions held in Hicks's Hall in January 1641 are given in the session roll. Those named were clearly considered to be the most important people present and several were well versed in the law: Sir Robert Hyde, knight and Chief Justice; Sir John Keeling, knight, of the Court of Common Pleas; and Sir Robert Atkins K.B. who was the Queen's solicitor. There were also Sir John Robinson, knight and baronet who was Lieutenant of the Tower and four other baronets, five knights and one esquire along with an unstated number of 'other justices.'

Two Middlesex Sessions each year were held in Westminster, somewhere within the Abbey precincts. Westminster had its own Commission of the Peace from 1618 until 1844, but Middlesex justices were eligible to be included in both commissions. Extant records of the Westminster sessions run from 1689.

At the Sessions of the Peace the Middlesex justices inquired 'on the oaths of good and lawful men' into the matters brought before them and took a preliminary view as to the seriousness of the offence, dealing with minor matters summarily, but if in doubt submitted the facts to a Grand Jury. If a 'true bill' (what might nowadays be called 'a case to answer') was found the matter went to the next Commission of Gaol Delivery. The

[1] Middlesex Sessions Records, New Series,Vol 1, p.9.
[2] Middlesex County Records, Vol IV, pp.345-6.

offender was either granted bail with sureties or was kept in Newgate, the common gaol of the City of London and the county of Middlesex.

The Commission of Oyer and Terminer was granted to royal judges, the Lord Mayor and aldermen and to some (not all) Middlesex justices. The Commission held a similar inquest on oath and the prisoner, if indicted, appeared before the Commission of Gaol Delivery.

At the Commission of Gaol Delivery the prisoner either pleaded guilty and was sentenced or 'put himself on the country', i.e. he or she elected to be tried by jury. The sessions records contain lists of suitably qualified freeholders who were eligible to serve on a jury.

The Commission of Gaol Delivery came to an end in 1834 with the establishment of the Central Criminal Court at the Old Bailey. After the closure of Newgate Prison in 1902, the present Old Bailey, designed by E W Mountford, was built on the site. It was opened in 1907 and has since been extended.

People from the Uxbridge area appearing at the Middlesex Sessions
Middlesex justices dealt with many local people at Clerkenwell and at the Commission of Gaol Delivery.

Benefit of clergy
Some prisoners claimed benefit of clergy. This was a medieval form of immunity from punishment by the ordinary courts of law that was originally bestowed on 'literate' clergy, but later extended to anyone at all who could recite from memory the first verse of the 51st Psalm - or 'neck verse' as it became known. Both 'clergyable offences' and the range of people who could claim the benefit were gradually reduced and a rule was introduced preventing it being claimed twice over. It was abolished in 1827. The following are examples:

March 1573: William Welles, late of London, Clerk, stole at Woxbridge a linen smock and a linen sheet worth three shillings and a linen napkin and a linen partelett (a ruff) worth 12 pence. He pleaded guilty, but produced letters from the Bishop of Llandaff certifying that he was a clerk in Holy Orders. The letters were accepted by the court and instead of being sentenced to be hanged, he was handed over to the Ordinary (i.e. the local bishop) because clerks in Holy Orders were exempted from criminal process before secular judges.[3] Welles would have been kept in the Bishop's Prison – the Bishop of London had a prison beside his palace at St Paul's at this period – until being allowed to make his purgation. That is, he would have to swear his innocence (although he had pleaded guilty) and produce 12 compurgators to back his word. William Welles really was a clerk in holy orders, but generally the ability to read 'in a clerkly manner' was accepted as proof. An Act of 1488/9 restricted benefit of clergy in respect of people who were not actually in holy orders so that it could only be claimed on a single occasion. Those claimants who were guilty of murder were branded, often on the thumb, with an M for murder, or with a T for Tyburn[4] in respect of any other felony, to mark them out permanently. The branding was done by a gaoler in front of a judge prior to the prisoner being turned over to the ordinary. After another Act in 1575/6 those who had successfully read their 'neck verse' (above) were freed immediately after branding, unless the judge considered this too lenient, in which case they could be imprisoned for up to a year.

June 1613: John Samon a yeoman of Uxbridge broke 'burglariously' into Michael Page's house at eleven o'clock at night and stole silver salts worth £13 13s 4d. He was found not guilty of the burglary, but guilty of the felony, but he 'asked for the book, read it and was burnt' (branded).[5]

December 1624: Henry Marke, a labourer from Harefield, having stolen six cows worth three pounds each from Lady Alice, Countess of Derby, widow, successfully 'sought the book, read like a clerk and was sentenced to be branded'.[6] Lady Alice lived at Harefield Place, where the Australian War Cemetery is today.

In the reign of James I (1603-25) literacy was increasing with the spread of grammar schools and charity schools and 39 per cent of those sentenced to death escaped the gallows by reading like a clerk.[7]

---

[3] Middlesex County Records, Vol I, pp.80-1.

[4] After the London place of execution, Tyburn Tree, near the present Marble Arch.

[5] Middlesex County Records, Vol II, p.88.

[6] Ibid Vol II, p.186.

[7] Middlesex County Records, Vol II, pp. xxxviii-xxxix.

4 June 1573: At Woxbridge Thomas Shoones late of Harmondsworth, yeoman, stole a brown gelding worth 20 shillings of the goods and chattels of Thomas Doo. Two other cases of horse stealing were on the file, at Harmondsworth on 12 August and at Cowley on 8 September. He pleaded guilty and was sentenced to be hanged.[8] Either Thomas Shoones was illiterate or, since he had a previous conviction, he may have already pleaded his benefit of clergy on the earlier occasion.

Initially, benefit of clergy did not extend to women, but a statute of James I accorded to women the benefit of their sex with respect to larcenies not exceeding the value of ten shillings.[9]

Transportation

Some felons were granted a reprieve by being sent to British colonies – the Bermudas, Virginia after 1607, Jamaica and in later times Australia and Tasmania – sometimes for a period of seven or ten years, or maybe even for life. Shipmasters were contracted to carry a number of prisoners and to bargain with plantation owners abroad for prisoner's services for the duration of their sentence. Roger Lovejoy and Thomas Somervell, having been found guilty of stealing a bay gelding, were sentenced to be hanged in 1649, but the words 'Repr. Pro Virginia' appear after their names. An accomplice was still at large.[10] In the mid-seventeenth century there was also a spate of kidnappings with the victims being sold abroad. In November 1655 Christian Chacrett (a woman) had to answer the complaint of Dorothy Perkins

> who accuseth her for a spirit one that takes upp men woemen and children and sells them a-shipp to bee conveyed beyond the sea, having intised and inveigled one Edward Furnifull and Anne his wife with her infant to the waterside and put them aboard the ship called *The Planter* to be conveyed to Virginia.[11]

---

8 Ibid Vol I, p.88.
9 Middlesex County Records, Vol II, p.313.
10 Middlesex County Records, Vol III, p.283. Also during the mid-seventeenth century some Londoners sailed to the colonies as indentured servants. The poor were encouraged to do this to ease the burden on the rates.
11 Middlesex County Records, Vol I, p.239.

The War of American Independence put an end to transportation to America in 1775 and the resulting vastly overcrowded prisons had to be relieved by the use of 'hulks' (old ships stripped down and moored on the River Thames). Prisoners were sent to Australia from 1786. Those awaiting transportation were often first lodged in the hulks, sometimes for considerable periods of time. Charles Lamb from Ruislip who was found guilty of larceny in June 1838 and sentenced to seven years transportation, but he was kept in the hulks for the whole period of his sentence until his early release in 1844.[12] Transportation came to an end in 1868.

Matters arising before the justices at the Sessions of the Peace
The following is paraphrased from the archives:

April 1616, William Goodwyn of Uxbridge was indicted for stealing nine yards of canvas worth five shillings, belonging to Matthew Bates, a glover, in the town. He was found guilty to the value of 11d, had no goods to be seized and was sentenced to be whipped.[13]

This undervaluation of stolen goods was a merciful device used by the justices to avoid offenders being convicted of a felony and facing automatic capital punishment under England's Bloody Code. Only the previous year, William Goodwyn was accused of stealing a brass pot from Joan White, but nothing seems to have come of it. She may have decided not to give evidence against him. She was herself in Newgate by March 1616 because of her association with one Dionise Niccolls. There seems to have been trouble between three Uxbridge women in 1615. Redith White, wife of a chandler, had to keep the peace towards Sarah Hunt. Her husband and Richard Hallsey stood surety for her. Sarah Hunt had to keep the peace towards Alice Hackman with her husband and Francis Pitman as sureties.

Apprenticeship
If an apprentice wished to be free of his indentures he could seek an order of discharge from the justices. The justices freed many boys and girls who were being whipped and beaten without mercy, but the following local case is particularly dreadful. In October 1655 Mathew Nicholas was

---

[12] Celia Cartwright: Personal communication.
[13] Middlesex Sessions Records, New Series, Vol III, p.219.

discharged from his apprenticeship to William Lovejoy of Uxbridge, an edge tool maker. Mathew's father complained:

> that the said William Lovejoy employed his said apprentice on the Lord's Day at severall tymes in goeinge for money due to the said master, sometimes two, three, four, fyve or sixe myles from home, in gatheringe of wood and fewell upon the same day, and that the said master did very much misuse his said apprentice by fasteninge of a lock with a chaine to it, and tyinge and fetteringe him to the shoppe and that the said master his wife and mother did most cruelly and inhumanely beate his said apprentice, and also whip'd him until he was very bloody and his flesh rawe over a great part of his body, and then salted him, and held him naked to the fyre being soe salted to add to his paine'.[14]

Although William Lovejoy lost his apprentice and had to return half the indenture fees and the boy's clothes, the records are silent as to any action being taken against him for assault or cruelty.

In 1706 when another Uxbridge apprentice, Samuel Sells, bound to John Lock, a tallow-chandler and grocer, was freed because his master had given him immoderate correction, we are spared the harrowing details.[15]

Maintenance of children

In 1615 the justices ordered Roger Raynor, a fishmonger of Uxbridge, to pay for 'a bastard child begotten by him on the body of Margaret Weedon'. A tanner from Uxbridge and a cooper from Denham were sureties to see that he complied with the order.[16]

Jurors

A list of 25 jurors was drawn up in April 1616, from which 12 men were sworn to try Thomas Sampson and Thomas Harper for treason. Six of the men on the list were from Uxbridge and two of them, Thomas Burbeck and William Newberrie, were among those who found the two men guilty. Thomas Harper had clipped coins and was sentenced to be drawn upon hurdles up to the gallows at Tyburn (as opposed to travelling standing upright in a cart) and there to be hanged. Thomas Sampson who had

---

[14] Middlesex County Records, Vol III, p.239.
[15] Middlesex County Records, Sessions Books 1689-1709, p.305.
[16] Middlesex Sessions Records, New Series, Vol III, p.28.

counterfeited a licence to beg in the name of the king and even worse, the Great Seal affixed to it, faced a stiffer penalty; 'to be drawn and hanged, and his head to be cut off and his entrails burnt in the fire'.[17]

Recusants

According to the Recusancy Act 1581, everyone over the age of 16 who refrained from attending at church, chapel or some usual place of common prayer, if convicted, had to forfeit £20 per month. Among local recusants at that time were Anne Chapman, wife of William Chapman of Hayes, Juliana Byrd, wife of William Byrd, the well-known Elizabethan composer who lived in Harlington and three members of the Eden family of Ruislip.[18] John Eden had lost his job as an attorney at the Guildhall because of recusancy and had been arrested following the search of a house near Uxbridge in 1581.[19] In many cases the wife was the one who did not go to church. Sometimes the men were covert Catholics and attended divine worship in the local parish church to avoid punitive fines. William Byrd was a Catholic and was indicted as a recusant on various occasions, but not so frequently as Juliana. Although long lists of recusants are named as not attending church, there is no reference to any punishment in the seventeenth century, and it may be that as they were regarded as suspicious characters, a register was being kept so that constables could keep an eye on them.

Henry Garnet, Jesuit Superior of the English Province, lived at Moorcroft on Harlington Road in 1597. The house was afterwards owned by Robert Catesby (1573-1605).[20] Both men were executed after the Gunpowder Plot was frustrated. Moorcroft is known to Uxbridge residents (and in particular local magistrates) as a place used by Hillingdon Social Services for many years. Sir Robert Ashby (1563-1618) of Breakspears, who was a Middlesex justice, was fined for harbouring a Jesuit priest in 1604, but the State Papers give no further information.[21] Neither is there any reference to this affair in the Middlesex Sessions Records.

---

[17] Middlesex Sessions Records, Vol III, New Series, pp.224-6.

[18] Middlesex County Records, Vol I, p.123.

[19] Victoria County History, Middlesex Vol IV, p.91.

[20] Caraman, Philip, *John Gerard: The Autobiography of an Elizabethan* (2006), pp.246-7.

[21] National Archives, Cal SP dom, 1603-10, 151.

Moorcroft

Protestant dissenters

Uxbridge was a particularly strong centre of dissent in the seventeenth and eighteenth centuries with seven conventicles of Quakers and Presbyterians listed in the town in 1669.[22] They were persecuted in varying degrees, suffering acts of vandalism such as soldiers breaking furniture in their meeting rooms, being fined and sometimes imprisoned. Richard Richardson, who was himself a Quaker, kept the George Inn in Uxbridge, where the Friends met, and was fined £120 in 1684.[23] He moved away to farm in Harefield, and was involved in establishing the Meeting House in Uxbridge in 1691. The Act of Toleration, passed in 1689, permitted greater freedom of worship for Protestants. Justices issued certificates for certain houses to be used for worship. Houses belonging to Richard Hale and Edmund Blunt were certified as places of assembly in 1702 and Rice Davies's house in 1707. See also the notes below the picture on p.30.

Coroners' inquests

In December 1586 a coroner's inquest was held in Uxbridge on the body of John Bradley.[24] Five men had been fighting together in the highway at Uxbridge with swords and staves, 'when there came thither the aforesaid John Bradley in order to preserve the Queen's Peace'. He closed with Richard Atkyns. Robert Ingledon, a miller, seeing them fighting together

---

[22] *Old Meeting Congregational Church Uxbridge 1662-1962* (1962), Pearce, Kenneth R.
[23] *The Story of Uxbridge Quakers from 1658* (1970), Trott, Celia.
[24] Middlesex County Records, Vol I, pp.168-9.

struck John Bradley on the head with 'a coulstaffe, causing him to die instantly. The verdict was murder by Robert Ingledon.

In 1628 an inquest was held at West Drayton on 'an infant half a year old', where the child, Edward Fisher, was 'lying dead and slain'. Alice Gates of the same parish had assaulted him with a hatchet. She pleaded guilty to murder and was hanged.[25]

Highways and bridges

13 July 1644: a writ was addressed to William Turner, gentleman, one of the High Constables of Elthorne Hundred, to see that the highway surveyors of Ickenham make return to the justices at Hicks's Hall, by nine o'clock in the morning on 'Friday next' of the names of those who have repaired and those who have not repaired the highways.[26]

19 February 1617: an order was made for the repair of the High Bridge in the parish of West Drayton during a period of litigation between parishioners and Lord Paget who owned the manor. The inhabitants of West Drayton had to repair the bridge from time to time and Lord Paget should provide the timber for so doing 'as his ancestors before him have done and as his Lordship offered in Courte by his Counsell'.[27]

Alehouse licence

20 July 1610: Sir Robert Ashby and Christopher Merik, Esq. JPs took recognizance of Humphrey Hillman of Uxbridge, who was permitted to keep a common alehouse for one year at the 'Sign of the Spred Eagle' and was bound for the sum of £10 to observe the following conditions. He was not to allow the playing of 'cards, dice, tables, quoits, loggets, scailes, bowles' or other unlawful games on his premises, nor to harbour 'rogues, vagabonds, sturdye beggars, masterless men or other suspected person or persons'. He was not allowed to sell beer during the hours of divine service and could not serve meat during Lent.[28]

---

[25] Middlesex County Records, Vol III, p.21.
[26] LMA: Acc 312/11 (Tarleton Collection).
[27] Middlesex County Records, Vol I, p.126.
[28] National Register of Archives, Exhibition Catalogue, Uxbridge, April-May 1950.

Petition re church repairs

1 October 1629: The steeple of St John's, Hillingdon had become 'weak and decayed in the foundation walls', despite efforts by the parishioners to keep it in good repair. The Chancellor of the Bishop of London had ordered them to 'take it down and build it anew'. It was going to cost £800, but because most of the parishioners were 'but farmers at Rack Rents and poor men' they had only managed to contribute £200. They petitioned the justices to recommend their cause to the Lord Keeper of the Great Seal so that they could have their cause preached about and collections (briefs) made in churches. Sir Edmund Spencer and four other justices visited St John's and having viewed the steeple, found the cost reasonable and granted the parishioners a certificate from quarter sessions testifying to the genuineness of the facts alleged.[29]

Market regulations

The market at Uxbridge was essential to the economy of the town. All the London markets and many others had regulations to prevent forestalling, regrating and engrossing, offences which involved buying up quantities of a commodity by middlemen and reselling at a higher price. However, some movement and resale of goods was necessary and men known as 'badgers' and 'kidders' in all parts of Middlesex were granted licences by the justices to do this. In 1615 in the west of the county there were seven badgers in Harmondsworth, one from Feltham, five from Pinner, one from Teddington, one from Hammersmith, two from Ealing, one from Hounslow, eight from Heston, five from Hillingdon, one from Uxbridge, four from Hanwell, two from Cranford and one from Ruislip.[30]

The very high price of corn caused the Middlesex justices some concern in 1709 and all justices in the county were summoned to an inquiry to be held in the Exchequer Chamber at Westminster. Three local justices, Thomas Franklyn of Hayden Hall, Eastcote, Mr Hawtrey of Eastcote House, Colonel Shoreditch of Ickenham and Mr Jennings were especially desired to be present 'as they have information and knowledge of great misdemeanours committed in Uxbridge Market touching the engrossing of corn there.' As a result of the inquiry, orders were made to

---

[29] National Register of Archives, Exhibition Catalogue, Uxbridge, April-May 1950, pp.12-13.

[30] Middlesex Sessions Records, New Series, Vol II, pp. 293-4.

prevent farmers holding back corn from the markets and selling it by sample.

Middlesex Sessions House, Clerkenwell Green

Clerkenwell Sessions House

Hicks's Hall was in such a bad state of repair by the 1770s that a new sessions house was considered necessary. A rather heavy, but handsome building was designed by John Rogers and built at the western end of Clerkenwell Green, close to the bank of the River Fleet (which now flows through a pipe below Farringdon Road). It is still standing and is now a Masonic centre. It opened in 1782 with a fine Jacobean fireplace from Hicks's Hall incorporated into one of the rooms. While the new sessions house was being erected, the justices were offered the use of the Guildhall in King Street, Westminster, by the Duke of Northumberland, lord lieutenant of the County, where the Westminster justices already met.

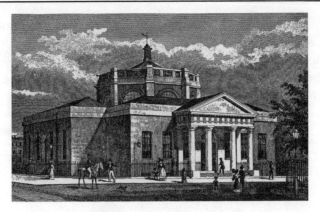

Westminster Guildhall 1805-92

Westminster Guildhall 1892-1911

With the formation of the county of London in 1889, the sessions house at Clerkenwell Green was no longer in Middlesex, but in the new county. Justices of the Westminster Commission were transferred to the Commission for the County of London. The Clerkenwell Sessions House was handed over to the London County Council (LCC) and in return the second Westminster Guildhall (built 1808) in Little Sanctuary, Westminster, was sold to the Middlesex County Council for £10,000 for use as a sessions house and as a county hall. Legislation transferred most of the remaining local government duties of the justices to the new county councils and two floors were added to the existing Guildhall to accommodate the new offices. Presumably this building was not sufficiently splendid for the new county council and a beautiful and highly decorative Guildhall was erected between 1911 and 1913 in Parliament Square to the designs of J S Gibson. Quarter Sessions were held there until 1972, when, along with Assizes, they were superseded by the Crown Court system under the Courts Act 1971.

The Old Meeting House in Beasley's Yard that was built in 1716 by a group of Presbyterian dissenters, descended from the conventicles (said to be in Uxbridge in 1669). The meeting became Congregational in 1833. The building was extended in 1883. Services have been held at nearby Christ Church since 1972 when the Old Meeting joined with the Methodists. In the early-1960s, the premises served as a temporary courtroom (p.80). It is now called Watts Hall and used for community purposes.

A warrant officer at Uxbridge Magistrates' Court in Victorian times

CHAPTER 3

Prisons and Bridewells

From 1553 onwards there was a separate place of detention for rogues, vagabonds and petty offenders. Edward VI had given the royal palace of Bridewell, built by his father, to be a workhouse for the City, but part of it became a house of correction. Here young offenders and vagabonds were put to work, in the hope of their rehabilitation and 'amendment', although the regime seems to have been mainly punitive. By the late seventeenth century there was little difference between the regimes in houses of correction and prisons, but the former were always the responsibility of local justices. Bridewell was used by both the City and the Middlesex justices. The name thereafter became associated with houses of correction and many were known as 'bridewells'. Refractory women and prostitutes were often sent to them and in some places the term 'bridewell' was used specifically to signify a women's prison.

The Clerkenwell House of Correction or Bridewell

Soon after Hicks's Hall was built, the Middlesex justices determined to build a new House of Correction for Middlesex to ease the overcrowding in Bridewell. On 21 October 1614, the justices decided that £2,000 should be raised by levying a rate upon the whole county. The amount to be raised from each place is listed in the Sessions Records.[1] The assessments for the Hundred of Elthorne, which included much of what is now the Borough of Hillingdon, were:

New Brainforde	£20	Woxbridge	£20
Hanwell	£12	Hillingdon	£45
Greenforde and Perryvall	£24	Rislippe	£50
Northall	£24	Harfield	£15
Southall alias Norwoode	£24	Ickenham	£12
Heyes	£40	Harmondesworthe	£12
Cranford	£6	Cowley	£10
Harlington	£36	West Drayton	£20

[1] Middlesex County Records, Vol II, pp.103-4.

The assessment had to reflect the size and rateable value of the various areas, but no rate is ever popular and some ratepayers railed at the cost of providing what may have been regarded as unnecessarily comfortable accommodation for prisoners. Michael Shorditche, lord of the manor of Ickenham, who lived at a house now called Manor Farm off Long Lane, uttered 'unfitt and mutinous language' saying that 'the county would withstand the rate'.[2] He was bound over for his future good behaviour in the then hefty sum of £100, an amount which he would surely have been loath to forfeit.

The House of Correction for Rogues and Vagabonds was opened within the year. A governor was appointed in October 1615 and a 'discreet woman' was to be appointed as matron and governess of the women, who were 'to be kept separate from prisoners of the other sex, in seven rooms especially assigned in the building to female prisoners.'[3] It was also known as the Clerkenwell Bridewell and stood between Corporation Row and Sans Walk. The establishment burnt down in 1679 and was rebuilt. It was considered deplorable by John Howard, the prison reformer, in 1757, and was demolished in 1804. By that time it had become redundant, as a new house of correction had been built in Coldbath Fields in 1794. The Post Office depot at Mount Pleasant is now on the site of Coldbath Fields. Uxbridge magistrates were sending offenders there in the 1850s for simple larceny (now theft). In the year to September 1856 they sentenced 12 males to hard labour for terms varying from seven days for stealing half a quartern loaf worth four pence to six weeks for taking eight cloth caps worth five shillings.[4]

Westminster Bridewell
Another bridewell was erected for Westminster in Tothill Fields, where Westminster Cathedral stands now, in 1618. It was rebuilt in 1834, and like Coldbath Fields, was an institution used by the Uxbridge magistrates. They sentenced a woman to six weeks with hard labour there in 1855 for stealing a shawl worth 16 shillings and 15 shillings in money.[5] The Westminster Bridewell was closed in 1885.

---

[2] Middlesex County Records, Vol II, pp.105-6.
[3] Middlesex County Records, Vol II, pp.117-8.
[4] LMA: PSU1/1.
[5] LMA: PSU1/1.

Vagrants

Many of the people sent to the houses of correction (or bridewells) in the sixteenth, seventeenth and eighteenth centuries were vagrants. The laws against them were excessively rigorous and constantly changed as governments struggled to control the social problems caused by mobile and 'masterless' men. The homeless wanderers could be branded with a letter V for vagabond or an R for rogue for a first offence and a second offence constituted a felony if the offender were over 18. Such felons could be hanged unless they were taken into employment for two years by someone who would guarantee their good behaviour. This was a form of slavery. We see the law in action in the case below:

> *26 July 1575:* True Bill that, whereas Joan Wynstone, Elizabeth Hopkyns and Margaret Archer on the 6th of February last past, were convicted of vagrancy and sentenced to be whipt and burnt on the gristle of the right ear with a hot iron of a thumb's circuit, the same Joan, Elizabeth and Margaret, being each of them over eighteen years of age, on the aforesaid 26th of July were vagrants at Clarkenwell co Midd. and other places in the same county.

Joan and Margaret pleaded guilty, but Elizabeth insisted that she was not guilty. Margaret was committed to the service and custody of John Luck of Wickeham, Bucks, yeoman, for the space of two years, the said John being bound in his own recognizance in the sum of ten pounds to produce the same Margaret at the Session of the Peace on expiration of the said term, or else to provide sufficient proof of her death. Joan Wynstone's husband came forward and took her into his own service for two years, standing surety for ten pounds. The story does not end there. Both Margaret and Joan removed themselves from their custodians without permission in the October following. They pleaded guilty but claimed to be pregnant. A jury of matrons found that Margaret was with child and she was remanded, but Joan Wynston was declared to be not pregnant and forthwith sentenced to be hanged.[6] From time-to-time a list of the names of 'matrons' appears in the Sessions Records, but with no information about their qualifications.

Following an act of 1597/8, vagrants were whipped and then passed via parish constables to the place where they had last resided for a whole year. The expenses were borne by the parishes through which they passed.

---

[6] Middlesex County Records, Vol I, pp.101-2, 103.

An Act of 1699 placed the burden on the county rather than the parish and because of mounting expenses in the eighteenth century, Middlesex justices, from 1757 onwards employed a vagrancy contractor. He cleared bridewells of vagrants twice a week and took them to pass houses where they were confined until constables in a neighbouring county took over responsibility - at South Mimms, Ridge, Enfield, Colnbrook and Staines.

The New Prison

At the end of the seventeenth century, a prison called 'The New Prison' was erected alongside the Clerkenwell Bridewell as 'an ease to Newgate', which was constantly overcrowded. The insanitary conditions had all too often led to inmates dying before coming to trial. This fate befell Dionise Nicolls of Uxbridge in 1616 (also mentioned in *Chapter 2*). She was said to have stolen a ruff, a gold ring, an ell of cambric, a silk girdle, a silver thimble, two pairs of gloves, two handkerchieves, an apron, two purses, a stomacher, a pair of stockings, a smock, a napkin, a pair of silk garters, a silver point, a box, a quarter of a yard of gold lace, a cross-cloth, ten pearls and a purse with 26d of money in it – all belonging to John Heydon of Iver. Perhaps he was a haberdasher travelling through Uxbridge, which is where the theft took place. The goods were worth £3 15s 2d (stealing goods worth more than one shilling constituted a felony) and had Dionise Nicolls been tried and found guilty she would have been sentenced to be hanged. However, Joan White, who was accused of receiving the stolen goods and helping her, was luckier, surviving the 'pining sickness' or gaol fever (typhus) that afflicted so many in Newgate. Eventually, having nothing proved against Joan White, she was freed.[7]

The New Prison was rebuilt in the 1770s, only to be attacked during the Gordon Riots in 1780. In 1818 it was enlarged and enclosed as well as the site of the former bridewell, a pleasure ground adjoining called the Mulberry Garden and the site of a former workhouse, which the Middlesex justices had used as 'a Colledge of Infants' for a few years in the late seventeenth century.[8] The Victorians, who believed in well-designed and hygienic prisons, took the prison down and rebuilt it for the Middlesex justices in 1845 to a plan by the county surveyor, William Moseley, similar

---

[7] Middlesex Sessions Records, New Series, Vol III, p.223.

[8] Senate House Library: 2645 ('An Account of the General Nursery or College of Infants set up by the Justices of the Peace for the County of Middlesex').

to that of Pentonville Prison.[9] It was called the House of Detention as it was intended for prisoners awaiting trial.

A hole was blown in the prison wall, houses opposite destroyed, six people killed and 50 more injured in 1867, during the so-called 'Clerkenwell explosion', when friends of Irish Fenian prisoners set off a barrel of gunpowder against the wall to try to effect their escape. The main perpetrator, Michael Barrett, was the last person in Britain to be hanged in public.[10] This prison was closed in 1877. The Hugh Middleton School was built on the site in 1893. During Queen Victoria's reign several new prisons had been built in the London area.

The conditions inside the prisons and bridewells were at all times appalling, partly due to overcrowding and poor sanitary arrangements, but mainly owing to the system of management. The prison keepers usually had no salary, or at times a very small one, and were expected to make a profit by putting prisoners to work (such as beating hemp and picking oakum). There was no allowance for the sustenance of prisoners, who were expected to buy their own food or have it provided by friends. The vagrants packed into the bridewells were usually penniless and friendless and as whole families were often vagrant, there were many babies and children inside as well as adults. Their distress was acute. Large numbers died and although coroners did hold some inquests in prisons, many deaths were not properly examined. Charitable attempts to succour prisoners were swamped by the huge demand for assistance. Justices were occasionally so moved by the stories they heard that they put their hands into their own pockets, reminding the present writer that as recently as 2002 there was a Poor Box at Uxbridge courthouse to assist impecunious offenders who had no money for 'bus, coach or train fares to get home.'

The Middlesex justices held an inquiry in August 1741 into conditions in the House of Correction.[11] Relatively few inquests were being held because it was found that coroners were charging heavy fees – 13s 4d for themselves and six and seven shillings for the jury – which had to be paid out of the keeper's pocket. Prisoners were in a starving condition, too weak to get themselves into court, let alone work, although those that did work were said by the keeper to be able to earn between one penny half-penny

[9] *An Historical Walk Through Clerkenwell* (1980), Cosh, Mary, Islington Libraries.
[10] In 1868 outside Newgate Prison.
[11] Middlesex County Records: Reports 1902-1928, pp.97-100.

and two pence per day. He also claimed to give one quartern loaf a day between eight prisoners sentenced to hard labour, out of his own pocket. Charitable relief, in the form of broth, came from the Quakers who were running the workhouse next door to the Bridewell at that time. The justices decreed that an allowance of one penny per day per inmate should be defrayed by money raised by a county rate. In return more work should be demanded from each prisoner. Later the allowance was varied to one pennyworth of bread per day, to prevent the money being spent on Geneva (gin), that was causing havoc in Londoners' lives, as vividly depicted in Hogarth's *Gin Lane*. The justices further ordered that an inquest be held upon the death of any prisoner and that the coroner have no fee.

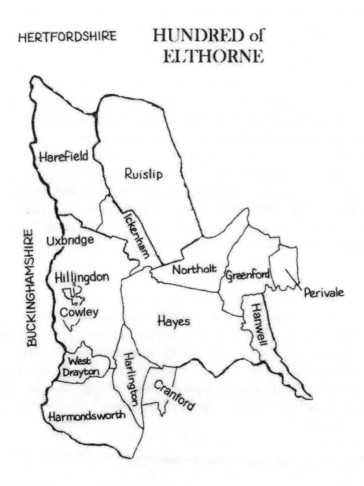

HERTFORDSHIRE HUNDRED of ELTHORNE

CHAPTER 4

Uxbridge Justices in the 18th and 19th Centuries

Middlesex had been divided into six hundreds (administrative areas) in Saxon times: Elthorne, Spelthorne, Hounslow, Gore, Edmonton and Ossulstone. Uxbridge had become the market town of Elthorne by the late twelfth century. Gilbert Bassett, Lord of the Honor of Wallingford, granted the burgesses the right to hold a market every Thursday and to collect tolls in a document dating from c.1170. Uxbridge occupied a strategic position where the London to Oxford road crossed the River Colne and the way to Windsor branched off to the south-west. The market was held where the roads diverged (now High Street and Windsor Street). Although the town had a chapel, St Margaret's, close to the market, it lay within the parish of St John's at Hillingdon on the hill-top above the river valley. The Hundred of Elthorne included the villages of Harefield, Ruislip, Ickenham, Cowley, Colham, Hillingdon, Hayes, West Drayton, Dawley, Hanwell, Harmondsworth, Harlington, Cranford, Northolt and Greenford.

Counties were divided into petty sessional areas as a result of an Act of Parliament passed in 1551 and Uxbridge was the natural meeting place for the Elthorne Division, but very little is known of actual proceedings as there are no extant petty sessional records until 1855. Prior to that some knowledge of the work of the local magistrates can be gleaned from passing references in the records of the sessions held at Clerkenwell and Westminster, newspapers and from parish documents relating to the working of the Poor Law. Justices in petty sessions usually dealt with bastardy, settlement and removals, breaches of the peace, and licensing. They also took examinations on oath as a preliminary investigation in very serious matters such as murder. Some, but not all local justices attended the general sessions where rates, the running of lunatic asylums and other county business were discussed and Quarter Sessions were held to deal with more serious or high level judicial matters. By the nineteenth century sessions were held almost continuously throughout the year at Clerkenwell and Westminster, general sessions and quarter sessions in alternate months.[1]

---

[1] LMA: Guides to court and sessional records.

Redford and Riches, in their *History of Uxbridge*, published in 1818, say that petty sessions had been held in Uxbridge 'upward of a century' on the first and third Mondays of each month 'to transact the public business of this place, and for the parishes in this Division: namely, Cowley, Cranford, West Drayton, Harlington, Harmondsworth, Harefield, Hayes, Hillingdon, Ickenham, Northolt and Ruislip.'[2] However, meetings had taken place earlier than that. Justices 'sitting at Uxbridge' in 1692 refused a victualling licence to Stephen Chipps of Hayes. Chipps, apparently knowing how to play the system, simply went to London where he was unknown and obtained one 'surreptitiously', but was found out and the matter went to sessions where his licence was suppressed.[3]

Settlement
Overseers of the poor sought to get rid of paupers who needed assistance from the rates by passing them back to their place of settlement (which depended, e.g. on matters such as place of birth, apprenticeship or being in service for a year and a day). Usually one or two justices examined the poor people on oath and made an order of removal if appropriate. Vestry books illustrate how mobile people were, even in an age of horse-drawn and relatively expensive transport, but never tell the whole human story behind the bare details recorded.

In March 1792 George Montague, resident in Ruislip, was examined by Thomas Bishop and William Evans JPs. He said that he had 'heard and believes he was born in Acton' and that his parents were legally settled there. At the age of seven he was put out as an apprentice by the churchwardens and overseers of Acton to John Montague of Ickenham, blacksmith, until he was 24 years old. His indentures were dated 16 April 1774. He married Ann Scaffold of Ruislip in 1790 and had an eleven-month-old daughter.[4] Churchwardens and overseers frequently apprenticed pauper children outside of their home parish so that they would gain settlement elsewhere. Such apprenticeships lasted until a boy was 24 regardless of the child's age at the outset. Pauper girls were apprenticed until the age of 21 or marriage if earlier. Male apprentices

2 *History of Uxbridge* (1818), Redford, G and Riches, T H, p.147.
3 In this context alcohol. Victuals were more generally refreshments. Middlesex County Records Session Books 1689-1709, p.73.
4 LMA: DRO 19/C1/7 (Vestry Memoranda Book).

could not marry. It looks as though George Montague had applied to the Ruislip overseers for assistance and they believed that his legal place of settlement was Ickenham. It is not known whether he had been apprenticed to a relative, which was not unknown, or had simply been given his master's surname.

Montague's smithy at Ickenham early twentieth century

March 1792: Joshia Kempton's tale was that he had been born in Great Hormead, Herts and was a collar-maker. He had rented a shop in Hampstead in 1782, where he had resided for seven years and paid £15 per annum rent and taxes 'and he has not done any act since whereby he has gained a settlement'. About ten years previously he had married Hannah Naylor at Ruislip church and had three children aged nine years, five years and nine months respectively. The justices ordered the removal of the Kemptons to Hampstead. The Ruislip overseers paid three shillings for a warrant, 5s 6d to the constable to escort the family and 10s 6d to James Dewe who presumably drove the horse and cart that conveyed them.[5]

May 1792: Ann Allday was Ruislip born, but had gone to London to work. In March 1791 she had hired herself to Mrs Ann Hitchen, pastry cook and confectioner at 21 The Strand at £6 per annum wages – a month's wages or

5 LMA: DRO 19/E1/1 (Overseers of Poor Accounts 1788-1808).

a month's warning.[6] She had continued there only 14 months before returning to Ruislip and was evidently seeking assistance from the overseers of the poor. The outcome of this case is not stated.[7]

Appeals against justices' orders went to Middlesex Sessions. Justices, Peter de Salis and Thomas Hussey ordered the removal of Sarah Bugbee and her five young children from Ruislip to Harrow-on-the-Hill on 15 February 1813. The churchwardens and overseers of the poor of Harrow-on-the-Hill addressed a petition 'to the Justices of the Peace in General Quarter Sessions assembled' because they were 'aggrieved by the order.' The churchwardens and overseers of the poor of Ruislip were informed on April 6 that they were to attend the Sessions House in Clerkenwell on April 8 at 'nine in the forenoon,'[8] which seems rather short notice.

Removals ceased in the 1830s with new methods of dealing with the poor brought in by the Poor Law Amendment Act 1834. The Act removed responsibility for the care of the poor from individual parishes and created unions, governed by the Poor Law Commission and later the Poor Law Board. The Uxbridge Union comprised Harefield, Ickenham, Ruislip, Northolt, Hillingdon, Cowley, Hayes, Norwood and West Drayton. Small parish workhouses such as had existed in Harefield, Ruislip, Northolt, West Drayton, Hayes, and Uxbridge, were closed down and sold to raise money for a large union workhouse. The Hillingdon parish workhouse was enlarged to become the union workhouse (Hillingdon Hospital is now on the site) and a board of Guardians ran the affairs of the union. Justices could sit on the board of guardians *ex officio.* The salaried clerk to the board was one Charles Woodbridge, a local solicitor.

Bastardy

Single women with babies proved expensive for parishes to maintain and efforts were made in the early nineteenth century to make the fathers pay, by way of bastardy orders. Such an order was made on 10 May 1813 and addressed to the constable of the parish of Ruislip. Sarah Tyler

hath by her voluntary examination, taken in writing on oath before me William Thompson Corbett Esq., one of His Majesty's Justices of the Peace...

---

6 LMA: DRO 19/C1/7 (Vestry Memoranda Book).
7 LMA: DRO 19/C1/7.
8 LMA: DRO 19/C1/7.

declared that about five weeks since she was delivered of a female bastard child in the workhouse of Ruislip now chargeable to the parish of Ruislip and that Markaram Bruce now or late of Chelsea College as a pensioner did beget the child on the body of her the said Sarah Tyler... and Daniel Deacon one of the Overseers of the Poor...in order to indemnify the parish ... hath applied to me to issue my warrant for the apprehending of the said Markaram Bruce and bring him before me or some other Justice to find security to indemnify the said parish or else to find a surety for his appearance at the next General Sessions of the Peace...[9]

Chelsea Pensioners were not necessarily old men.

Towards the end of the nineteenth century the Uxbridge justices' dealings with maintenance payments have some similarities to proceedings in the family proceedings court today. In 1897, under the heading 'Bastardy Arrears', Harry Ayres was committed to prison twice for failing to pay money to Elizabeth Byles, the mother of his child. He had served ten days in prison in April, and a warrant was issued in August, but was withdrawn, because an arrangement for payment was made. In September the matter was adjourned for a month and he was sent to prison for 28 days in October. Whether Henry Ayres could not pay because of his circumstances or wilfully refused to do so does not appear in the court register, but Elizabeth complained again in January 1898 and he was again committed for one month.[10]

Two violent deaths in 1839 – How local justices dealt with murder

Two deaths, one at a school in Hayes in March 1839, the other at a fish stall in Harefield in August of the same year, occurred after brief altercations between young men who were carrying knives and stabbed their opponents. On each occasion the perpetrator was taken into custody and the local justices began preliminary investigations, which were adjourned for an inquest to be held before Dr Thomas Wakley, coroner for West Middlesex. The inquest juries brought in verdicts of wilful murder against the accused in each case and the coroner tried to cut out any further investigation by the justices. On the first occasion the coroner issued a warrant for Francis Hastings Medhurst, who had stabbed Joseph Alsop in the belly at a private school at Wood End Green in Hayes, to be committed

---

[9] LMA: DRO 19/C1/7.
[10] LMA: PS/U1/12 (Court Register).

to Newgate immediately after the inquest. The justices were not pleased by this high-handed action and kept Medhurst in custody at Windsor Street police office, until they had completed their examination of witnesses.

The whole story emerges from the pages of *The Sunday Globe* and *The Times*. The trouble arose because Medhurst, aged 20, who had completed his studies but remained at the school as a boarder, had accused a pupil who had just left the room of breaking his watch glass. Joseph Alsop defended the other pupil's name. Several people witnessed the incident which took place in a classroom on a Saturday morning, including the headmaster the Reverend Frederick Sturmer. Mr Sturmer left the scene as soon as he saw Medhurst approach Alsop with a vine stick with a knob on it, obviously intending to attack him. He later excused his behaviour on the grounds that he thought that Joseph Alsop was going to get what he deserved – clearly a headmaster who believed that boys were best left to settle disputes themselves. Medhurst also had a knife, described variously in the accounts as 'a French knife', 'a Spanish dagger' and 'a life preserver' (a misnomer if ever there was one). After some provocation he stabbed Alsop in the belly. He then helped the victim to bed and a surgeon was called, who stitched the wound, apparently leaving the needle under the dressing. It was found to have rusted a couple of days later when another surgeon insisted upon uncovering the wound. Overcome by the result of his actions Medhurst, hovered around the sick room begging Alsop's forgiveness. Alsop is recorded as having said, 'We were both wrong. I forgive you', before dying on the following Thursday.

Medhurst meekly allowed himself to be taken by a teacher in a fly to Swakeleys, where a justice Thomas Truesdale Clarke lived. Rather oddly Mr Clarke said that he could not act until the coroner had been informed of the death and Medhurst and his escort were sent away, only to run into a horse patrol sent by another justice, Count de Salis, who lived nearer to the scene of the crime. Medhurst was conveyed to the police office in Windsor Street, Uxbridge. Messrs. Dagnall and Clarke, Count de Salis and Sir William Wiseman Bt, justices, examined witnesses upon oath at the Adam and Eve public house on the Friday and adjourned proceedings until the Monday. Meanwhile the inquest was held, also at the Adam and Eve, on the intervening Saturday and the coroner issued the warrant for Francis Medhurst's committal to Newgate, which the magistrates ignored.

According to a newspaper account the prisoner had remained in Windsor Street over the weekend, reading the bible and a prayer book assiduously, although offered the distraction of novels. Excitement ran high in Uxbridge and more than 100 people tried to cram into the small courtroom in the yard at the King's Arms on the Monday morning. The minutes of the examination have survived and are preserved at Uxbridge Library.[11] Counsel and a solicitor were present on behalf of Mr Medhurst, who was a man of property, and Mr Westron, a solicitor from Fenchurch Street, represented the aunts and guardians of the deceased.[12] After hearing all the facts and deliberating amongst themselves, the justices charged Medhurst with the lesser offence of manslaughter and committed him to sessions for a grand jury to look at the facts again. He was remanded to Newgate Prison and there was no application for bail.

The press printed some interesting background facts about Francis Medhurst. His grandfather had been convicted at the York Assizes in 1804 of killing his grandmother and in 1839 was resident at Moorcroft in Harlington Road, where Dr Stillwell kept a lunatic asylum.

Matters progressed with commendable speed. The death had occurred in mid-March and the sessions began on April 8. The grand jury found a true bill of manslaughter, but because of the inquest finding Mr Medhurst was tried on April 15 for wilful murder and manslaughter. The attorney-general for the defence, seeking manslaughter rather than wilful murder, cast aspersions on the ability of coroners with no legal training to direct a jury correctly and suggested that inquest juries, being composed of local people, were too much excited by the general hubbub surrounding thrilling cases to take a detached view. His client was convicted of manslaughter. The judge noted Francis Medhurst's remorse, the fact that he had acted in self-defence, his youth and the reprehensible behaviour of the headmaster and despite the fact that he carried a knife, sentenced him to three years in Coldbath Fields Prison, rather than seven years transportation.

Knife carrying seems to have been prevalent among local youths in the 1830s. George Coker, a 15-year-old Harefield boy had one on him when he went to buy fish from Moses Gates's stall. A quarrel arose over the price of fish and 21-year-old Moses Gates hit the boy three times before the knife

---

[11] Uxbridge Library: Museum Cupboard 266.
[12] Uxbridge Library: Museum Cupboard 266.

was drawn and Gates died from his wounds. The magistrates remanded Coker in custody to appear before them a few days later, an inquest to be held in the meantime and ordered that all the witnesses examined at the inquest should also appear before them. At the conclusion of the inquest, where a verdict of wilful murder was returned, Dr. Thomas Wakley took matters into his own hands. According to *The Times,* having refused to allow the prisoner to be taken again before the magistrates, he 'bound the constable of Harefield in the sum of £50 to deliver the accused forthwith at Newgate.'[13] The newspaper further reported that 'much interest was excited throughout the district as to the steps that would be adopted by the bench under the circumstances.' Apparently Mr Wakley, in the course of his remarks to the inquest jury, had 'made some very strong observations on the course adopted by the bench in pursuing the inquiry in the case of Mr Medhurst ... and said he should prevent the magistrates having the opportunity again.' No doubt fearful for his £50 the constable delivered the

Thomas Dagnall JP   Coroner Thomas Wakley

prisoner to Newgate on the morning that he should have brought him before the bench. The bench was non-plussed. George Coker, represented by Mr Chadwick-Jones, was found guilty of manslaughter at the Central Criminal Court and sentenced to transportation for life. The judge made the point that it was unmanly and 'unEnglish' to resort to a knife in every sudden quarrel and that it was the bounden duty of magistrates and judges to deal with such cases with great severity.

---

[13] *The Times* Digital Archive, August 1839.

The discrepancy between the sentences on Medhurst and Coker were commented upon in a letter to *The Times* and there was a general feeling that the younger boy had been unfairly treated, perhaps because of his lower social standing.[14]

This case demonstrates the rivalry between the justices and Thomas Wakley (1795-1862), who was a doctor, founder of *The Lancet,* a radical MP and social reformer. He had just been appointed coroner for West Middlesex in 1839. He insisted on holding inquests, normally considered unnecessary, on those who had died unexpectedly or by accident in prisons and workhouses and was well known for his belief that all coroners should be medically qualified. His inquests were often reported in some detail in *The Times* and he took every opportunity to publicise what he considered to be injustices caused by the new Poor Law. In this, he rubbed up against Charles Woodbridge, clerk to the board of Uxbridge guardians and also the clerk to the justices. Thomas Wakley leased Harefield Park, now Harefield Hospital, as his country residence from 1845 to 1856.

Removal of Mr C Morton Dyer from the Commission of the Peace[15]

There were further ramifications of the Medhurst case, which greatly exercised the Middlesex justices. At their meeting at Clerkenwell for the transaction of county business on 8 July 1841 a long discussion took place about the advisability of making public the reasons why one of their number, Mr C Morton Dyer, had been removed from the Commission of the Peace. Mr Dyer's name had already appeared in the press and there was much unwelcome speculation. Mr Dyer, when visiting the house of correction in February 1841, had met Francis Medhurst in a workshop, working as a wood turner. In conversation Mr Dyer, who was interested in wood turning, offered to suggest Medhurst's name for a new society that was being formed. There seem to have been several visits after that and Mr Dyer took an interest in the prisoner, who claimed to be very depressed by prison life, and promised to look into his case.

Francis Medhurst later told two prison chaplains and the governor that 'a person' had advised him that if he hoped for an early release he must be prepared to put up a large sum of money – £2000-3000. The 'person' was

[14] *The Times,* Digital Archive, Aug 17 1839.
[15] *The Times,* Digital Archive, 9, 10, 12 and 15 July 1841; 20 Aug 1841.

said to have mentioned a relationship between his own wife and the Marchioness of Normanby, wife of the Secretary of State for the Home Office, and also to have indicated that Lord Normanby himself and Lord Melbourne had authorised the offer and that if there were 'no play there would be no pay.' The chaplains and governor deduced that the 'person' must be Mr Dyer, whose animated conversations with Medhurst had been noted. The visiting justices held an inquiry behind closed doors and sent the results to Lord Normanby without any comment. The Lord Chancellor had then removed Mr Dyer from the Commission of the Peace because of 'indiscretionary conduct'.

Mr Dyer wrote to *The Times* (10 July 1841) claiming that the allegations were 'almost wholly untrue.' He stated that he had suggested to Mr Medhurst, who had recently come into an inheritance following the death of his grandfather in the asylum at Moorcroft, that he offer a large sum to a national charity 'to expiate in some measure the offence of which he had been found guilty' and thereby soften the adverse feelings of the public towards him. The letter from the Lord Chancellor and correspondence with Medhurst's solicitor were also published. An editorial (12 July 1841) exonerated Lord Normanby, but sensed some mystery. Three days later the newspaper reported Francis Medhurst's deteriorating state of health. He had been moved to the prison infirmary and the prison doctor and 'eminent members of the faculty' conjectured that he could not survive if kept incarcerated. A certificate to that effect had been sent to the Home Office. Medhurst was released on July 24, having served a little over two years of his three year sentence.

The whole affair had a shocking effect upon the Reverend Frederick Sturmer, who had been curate of Hayes as well as running his own private school. After the murder his life had been rendered miserable by people holding meetings, chalking on walls etc. and a group of parishioners had joined with dissenters in withholding their payments of the church rate. In February 1842 he appeared at an insolvent debtors' court. The case was adjourned and he was remanded in custody.

Nineteenth century improvements affecting the work of local justices

The nineteenth century has truly been called the 'age of improvement', with great strides forward in public health, transport, education and medicine and also with women beginning to emerge into public life, sitting on workhouse committees and school boards in the 1870s, but not on the bench until 1919.[16] The main improvements that affected the justices were changes in the Penal Code and the attitude towards criminals. At the end of the eighteenth century there were nearly 200 capital offences on the statute book, including planting a tree in Downing Street or impersonating a Chelsea Pensioner! By 1819 when Sir James Macintosh got a parliamentary committee of inquiry into the criminal laws, the number had risen to 223. When Robert Peel became Home Secretary in 1822 he drastically reduced the number, revised the punishments for lesser offences, improved conditions of imprisonment and looked for ways to prevent crime, not just punish it.

To this end he established the Metropolitan Police Force in 1829 and the Metropolitan Police District was extended to include Uxbridge and the surrounding area in 1840. A volunteer force set up in Uxbridge four years earlier with an office in Windsor Street was disbanded and the Metropolitan Police had a station provided on the corner of Uxbridge Road and Kingston Lane. They moved to a fine new police station in Windsor Street in 1871 (see the picture on p.50). When the police moved to their present police station in Warwick Place opposite to the Uxbridge courthouse in 1988, the Windsor Street building became a restaurant amusingly and aptly named 'The Old Bill'. It is now 'The Fig Tree'.

As a result of changing policies the pillory and stocks are heard of no more and whipping of adults became a thing of the past so far as the local courts were concerned, although retained as a punishment in prisons until 1948. Occasionally, Uxbridge magistrates ordered boys to be birched. In 1896-7 Bertie Hobbs aged 13 and eleven-year-old Joseph Springall were sentenced to six strokes each for stealing six shillings. A ten-year-old boy received five strokes for stealing cigarettes the following year.[17]

Matters dealt with by the justices in late Victorian times

The court registers provide the most meagre information: the name of the informant or complainant; the name of the defendant and his or her age if under 16; the nature of offence or matter of complaint; a minute of the adjudication and a note of the justices adjudicating. Nothing is said of the

---

[16] When women were also first given the vote. They joined the bench as a result of the Sex Disqualification (Removal) Act 1919.

[17] LMA: PS/U/12-13.

justices' reasons for imposing a particular sentence, but there were discernible patterns. For example drunks and defendants who were drunk and disorderly always received a five shilling fine or seven days custody, but being drunk whilst in charge of a horse and cart merited a 15 shilling fine or 14 days. Drunks formed the largest number of offenders in most years – 122 offences out of 263 in 1898.

Ruislip Workhouse   Harefield Workhouse

The offences dealt with in the 1890s reflect the still rural nature of the area and the smallness of the population. The total number of offences before the bench between June 1896 and December 1897 was only 389, compared with the hundreds every week nowadays. Courts were held once or twice a week. There were many market gardens, not just in Uxbridge, but in the Harmondsworth and Harlington area, so it is not surprising that stealing fruit was common. Young children, who may have merely been scrumping, were sometimes discharged, but eight-year-old Bertie Hobbs was fined one shilling for stealing walnuts, perhaps because he was going to sell them (schoolchildren collected acorns from local woods and sold them to farmers for their pigs). Stealing a duck earned a five shilling fine or five days, but stealing ferrets was dealt with much more severely with three months hard labour. Fines between 15 and 20 shillings and costs, usually 3s 6d or 4s 6d, but on one occasion £1 9s 6d, were imposed for cruelty to animals, mainly horses and ponies.

Uxbridge Police Station (right) (c.1982)

Other matters could have happened in any type of neighbourhood and are still common today. Larceny, unless very minor, meant imprisonment with hard labour, the term depending upon the value of the stolen property. Beggars (no longer called 'sturdy beggars') were often discharged. Six out of seven 'wandering lunatics', who appeared at court in 1855, were sent to the Uxbridge Union Workhouse and the other to Wandsworth Asylum. Lunatics who had been sent to the workhouse were presumably free to leave at will, much as other inmates came and went.

Assault was a frequent offence. George Darbon received the severest sentence in 1898, six months with hard labour for an attack on a policeman. John Sipperley's assault on a policeman must have been minor by comparison, as he was fined 15s 6d with 4s 6d costs. Some of the assaults on women were perpetrated by men with the same surname and were probably domestic incidents. Frederick Jones was fined for his assault on Matilda Jones, but the other domestic offenders were imprisoned with hard labour for periods of between ten days and three calendar months. In March 1898, William Dossett threatened to kill Ellen Dossett and was bound over for three months in the sum of £20 with one surety of £10 – 14 days in default. He assaulted her and William Henry Dossett, probably their son, four weeks later and was given two months hard labour and the 14 days to run consecutively. There were two charges of indecent assault in 1898, one against a boy of ten, who was discharged and another by an adult male who was also discharged on his second appearance. In the same year Rose Gibson accused two men of rape. Both charges were dismissed. She was before the bench for attempting to commit suicide in 1898, then a criminal offence. She was remanded for a week and was then sent to St Anne's House in Notting Hill.

There were no separate courts for juveniles until 1908. Sometimes quite young children were sent away from home for long periods of time. In 1896 the justices ordered an eleven-year-old boy, who was beyond the control of his parent, to the workhouse for one week and then to Ashford Industrial School until he was 16. Fourteen-year-old Ellen Birdsey, guilty of larceny, was sent to a reformatory for four years. Another 14-year-old, Sidney T Batten, charged with the serious offence of breaking and entering a dwelling house, was sent to the Middlesex Sessions.

Uxbridge Market House

CHAPTER 5

Magistrates and their Legal Advisers

The Middlesex justices from the rural parts of the county were drawn almost exclusively from the landed gentry. Some families were long established in the area and continued into the nineteenth and even into the twentieth century. The Ashbys had been at Breakspears since the 1440s, the Hawtreys and their descendants, the Rogers and Deanes, had lived at Eastcote House since the 1520s, whilst the Shoreditches had an even longer connection with Ickenham beginning in the mid-fourteenth century when they became lords of the manor. Commander A H Tarleton, who was tenuously descended from the Ashbys, sat at Uxbridge from 1891 to 1920 and Francis Henry Deane, owner of Eastcote House, sat as a magistrate until his death in 1892. The Breakspears estate at its largest was close to 700 acres.[1] The Eastcote House estate was nearly 1,000 acres around 1900.[2]

Commander Tarleton inherited Breakspears from a cousin in 1889 and came to live there a couple of years later, by which time he had left active service in the Royal Navy. He took an interest in archaeology and history. A number of historic documents, which he presumably found at Breakspears, are now in the London Metropolitan Archive.[3] One escaped and hangs on the wall of Retiring Room No.1 in the present Uxbridge courthouse. It is an impressment addressed to Robert Ashby Esq, 'by virtue of an Act for settling the Militia in England and Wales.' He is charged

> to provide and maintain there good serviceable muskets bandeleeros and swords which you are to bring or send by three fitt and able persons to the Signe of the Crowne in Woxbridge on Tuesday next being the 16th day of August instant by nine of the clock in the forenoon. To be then and there lifted for the service of the Commonwealth; and to be thenceforth in readiness upon command. Whereof you may not fail upon the penalties in the said Act mentioned.

---

[1] *Here and There in Harefield* (1989), Harefield Extra-Mural Local History Class, pp.12-22.
[2] *The Goodliest Place in Middlesex* (1989), Bowlt, Eileen M, p.146.
[3] Accession 312, Tarleton Collection.

Commander A H Tarleton JP

Thomas Truesdale Clarke JP

Francis Henry Deane JP

Robert Edward Master JP

Walter Barnard Byles JP

Charles Woodbridge

It is dated 13 August 1659 and signed 'Jo: Baldwin, John Readding, William Nicoll and William Turner, commissioners'.

Breakspears

Swakeleys

The times were unsettled because Richard Cromwell, Oliver Cromwell, the Lord Protector's son, had retired from office in April and Parliament was being controlled by a committee of army officers. Deputy lieutenants of counties administered the militia, but many justices were also deputy lieutenants and militia papers were always kept by the clerk of the peace. The yellowing cutting from the *Gazette* dated 1909 that accompanies the document, says that Mr Tarleton lent it to the petty sessions. It appears to have become a permanent loan.

The Clarkes of Swakeleys were comparative newcomers. The Reverend Thomas Clarke, rector of Ickenham, bought Swakeleys (see the picture on p.54), the park and deer and the lead pipes and conduit from a water house on Uxbridge Common for £7,100 in 1750, at the time of his marriage to Mary Blencowe of Hayes. His son, Thomas Truesdale Clarke (1774-1840) (p.53), grandson, Thomas Truesdale Clarke (1802-90) and great-grandson, William Capel Clarke-Thornhill (1832-98) all sat at the Uxbridge court. The first T T Clarke, filling in a questionnaire in 1834, said that he had been appointed 'about forty years ago' and that he was 'a barrister never having practised'.[4] The nature of his death was unfortunate. He appears to have suffered a mental breakdown in the spring of 1840. On a hot July afternoon he walked out of Swakeleys and across his park and fields toward Hercies. There were no roads between in those days. He was found drowned in the River Pinn, in just 20 inches of water, his body not being covered, only his face. The inquest was held at Swakeleys and the jury forebore to bring in a verdict of suicide, which had not in fact been proved, the coroner, Dr. Thomas Wakley, remarking that 'he thought it best not to stamp the family of the deceased with the stigma of insanity'. Clarke's son, according to an obituary in the local newspaper, enjoyed the life of a country gentleman and was 'the life and soul of many a merry party during the shooting season'. He also had a taste for amateur theatricals. His grandson, William Capel Clarke, married an heiress, Clara Thornhill, and he added her surname to his own. Although on the Uxbridge bench, he lived mostly on his wife's estates in Northamptonshire. The Swakeleys estate had grown under the Clarke stewardship and was 1,382 acres, including most of Ickenham, by 1922, when it was sold at auction and then largely developed.[5]

By the nineteenth century, however, several of the magistrates sitting at Uxbridge were newcomers to the area, having purchased their wide estates with money earned in business. The Cox family were well-known army agents and bankers at Craigs Court, Charing Cross. Richard Henry Cox, grandson of the founder of the firm, bought Hillingdon House for just

---

4 LMA: MJP/R/37.
5 Uxbridge Library: Auction brochure 1922.

under £30,000 in 1810 and joined the bench in 1822[6]. His son, Henry Richard Cox (1804-92) paid £110,000 for the Harefield Place estate in 1877 and, being unmarried, bestowed it upon his nephew, Frederick William Cox, who also joined the bench and died in 1913. At the time of his death the Harefield Place and Hillingdon House estates combined amounted to 2,547 acres and stretched from Mad Bess and Bayhurst Woods in Ruislip and Harefield to the village of Hillingdon.[7]

Hillingdon Court: Home of Lord Hillingdon and his far flung estates, now a school.

Harefield Place: Purchased by Henry Richard Cox in 1877, now offices.

Apart from being landlords of much of the area, there was a good deal of family and social interconnection between members of the local bench. Emily, daughter of Richard Henry Cox, married Charles Mills, another

---

[6] LMA MJP/R/46.

[7] Uxbridge Library: Auction brochure 1914

banker, in 1825 and they subsequently built Hillingdon Court (page 56) in Vine Lane. Their son, Charles Henry Mills, who sat on the Uxbridge bench, was created first Baron Hillingdon in 1886. Another of Richard Henry Cox's daughters married Algernon Greville, secretary to the Duke of Wellington. Colonel Arthur Charles Greville, their son, qualified as a Middlesex magistrate by virtue of a share in leasehold property in Lowndes Square in 1865 and sat at Uxbridge.[8] Although owning huge estates, the Cox men and the Mills attended to their business affairs in town as well. Lord Hillingdon's Hillingdon Court estate was the largest of them all, being 3,185 acres in 1920. It covered much of Hillingdon, Hayes and South Ruislip.[9]

The old established families played their part in improving the lives of their tenants in the nineteenth century, providing schools and institutes in the villages around Uxbridge and the Cox family played a part in establishing Uxbridge Cottage Hospital.

Dawley Court: Purchased by Jerome Count de Salis JP,
Later the home of Cecil Fane de Salis JP, Uxbridge bench chair (1921-31).

At that time, justices were appointed for life, but it is clear that they varied as to their interest in the work and their attendance. In 1887, 13 men were listed as justices for the Uxbridge Division.[10] Seven of them: Mr Clarke and Mr Clarke-Thornhill; Henry Richard Cox and Frederick Cox;

---

[8] LMA: MJP/QC/95 and MJP/R/210.
[9] Uxbridge Library; Auction brochure 1920.
[10] LMA: MJP/R/210.

Lord Hillingdon; William Fane de Salis and Sir Samuel Morton Peto; had not attended for a year. Peto, the railway engineer who had leased Eastcote House for some years, was said to have moved to Tonbridge, but no reasons were given for the other absences, although at 85 Thomas Truesdale Clarke may have been feeling his age. William Fane de Salis (1812-96) of Dawley Court (see the picture on p.57) was descended from a Swiss family that owned property around Dawley and Harlington and Hillingdon from the eighteenth century. His elder brother Peter de Salis (1799-1870) was a Count of the Holy Roman Empire and also sat on the Uxbridge bench.

The six men who sat regularly and were effectively the Uxbridge bench, were Francis Henry Deane, then living on Uxbridge Common at a house called East View; Colonel A C Greville of St Andrew's Common; R E Master Esq of Hillingdon Furze; W B Byles Esq. of Harefield House, C M Wakefield Esq. of Belmont and Ewald Mosley Esq. F H Deane, W B Byles and C M Wakefield (see amongst the various pictures on p.53) were all barristers-at-law, the last two being the sons of judges. Robert Master and Colonel Greville were the only ones who attended Quarter Sessions at Clerkenwell as well as petty sessions at Uxbridge.[11] It is notable that there is no record of clergymen on the Uxbridge Bench during the nineteenth century. Elsewhere they were active in the magistracy and formed 25 per cent of active magistrates in 1832.

Uxbridge justices and the game laws

Practically all justices in the country parts of Middlesex were landowners with game interests and they dealt with poachers vigorously according to the game laws. The Clarkes of Swakeleys were some of the justices who invested in the sporting facilities of their land, by planting coverts and employing gamekeepers. There were shooting parties every autumn and local schoolmasters bewailed the fact that many of the older boys were absent because they had joined the beaters. There was some tension between school teachers and justices. The Harefield schoolmaster entered his concerns in the school log book:

---

[11] LMA: MJP/R/226.

I have seen the attendance officer and he says it is useless taking them to court as the magistrates will not convict, and in cases where they do, the fine is so small, usually 1 shilling or 1s 6d, that they do not mind.

Poaching was another matter and the almost inevitable punishment was custody, especially in the 1840s and 1850s when it was rife because labourers were largely unemployed in the parts of the Uxbridge Union like Ruislip where there was virtually no employment other than on the land and where farming was at a low ebb. Brickfields in Hayes, Dawley and West Drayton provided alternative and better-paid work, though mainly on a casual basis, to people in those areas. Harefield labourers had opportunities for employment at the copper mills and at lime works. The farmers claimed that their income was affected by the preservation of game because the birds ate their crops. Despite knowing that putting the breadwinner of a family into prison for a few weeks increased the distress, the preservation of game was considered so important that the practice continued. Even so humane a landowner as Thomas Wakley who leased Harefield Park, prosecuted poachers, but supported their wives and families out of his own pocket during their period of incarceration.

Clerks to the justices at Uxbridge

The legal advisers who supported the justices became more professional in Victorian times. Local justices seem always to have employed clerks, sometimes solicitors, as personal assistants. The job was part-time because the courts met just once or twice a week and the clerks made what they could from fees charged for drawing up warrants, certificates and other documents. The Justices' Clerks' Society was formed in 1839 and from 1877 clerks to the justices received salaries. Charles Woodbridge (1796-1879) mentioned in *Chapter 4* in relation to the board of guardians, was clerk to the Uxbridge justices from the 1830s-1874. His son, Charles (1830-1924), followed him and died in office at the age of 94, being succeeded by his nephew, Algernon Rivers Woodbridge (1870-1951) who was clerk from 1924-46. Many 'old-style' justices' clerks had distinctive reputations due to the way in which they chose to discharge their duties. Laurance Henry Crossley who arrived at Uxbridge Magistrates' Court in 1946, after army service during the war years, is said to have ruled the court and all court users with a rod of iron. In 1982 he handed over to David Simpson who later became the first Uxbridge clerk to rise to the bench when he was appointed as one of a new breed of professional magistrates styled 'district judge (magistrates' courts)'. His successor, Martin Hamilton, was the first barrister justice' clerk at Uxbridge and the last such as the administrative arrangements changed with the arrival of the Greater London Magistrates' Courts Authority (GLMCA) in 2001.

Middlesex Guildhall c.1939 (now often referred to as Westminster Guildhall)

Middlesex County Council 1889

The Local Government Act 1888 brought about significant earlier administrative changes. County councils were set up which took over many of the civic duties formerly performed by JPs. Apart from licensing matters, all the old county business passed to paid county council officers, leaving the justices to deal almost entirely with judicial matters. Middlesex, already an oddity because the City of London and the Liberty of Westminster lay within its boundaries, was greatly diminished in size by the establishing of the entirely new county of London, which was carved out of Middlesex and Surrey. Justice was to be organized by a Standing Joint Committee. The Metropolitan Police then remained under the direct jurisdiction of the Home Office, so the Standing Joint Committee (SJC), which in most counties regulated the police, in Middlesex dealt with such matters as accommodation for the sessions. This led to the extension of the existing Guildhall at Westminster between 1889 and 1893, and in rapid succession to the rather extravagant brand new Guildhall built in

Parliament Square in 1911 (below).[12] The SJC also turned its attention to new accommodation for magistrates' petty sessional divisions. It was time for Uxbridge to have a properly designed court house.

Uxbridge Magistrates' Court 1913

---

[12] Now scheduled as the home of the UK's first Supreme Court from 2009: *Chapter 8.*

CHAPTER 6

'A Suitable Home for Justice'

The Middlesex Standing Joint Committee worked hard to provide the eight petty-sessional divisions in Middlesex with proper court houses from 1899 onwards. The Gore and Willesden Divisions were large enough to warrant two separate court houses each.[1] Gore had had a court house in Edgeware next door to the Chandos Arms and leased from Clutterbuck's brewery (not thought to be a happy situation for a magistrates' court) since 1850. It was replaced by a purpose-built courthouse at The Hyde in Hendon in 1913. The second courthouse was built at Wealdstone from 1905-09, linked by an arch to a new police station, at the expense of the Metropolitan Police[2] and designed by the police architect, J Dixon Butler. The Willesden courthouses were opened at Harlesden in 1899 and Acton in 1907. Others had been erected at Wood Green in the Edmonton Division, at Highgate (Highgate Division) and at Feltham in the Spelthorne Division, while court accommodation had been improved at Brentford (Brentford Division) and Staines (Spelthorne Division) town halls. South Mimms Division had to wait until 1913 for a new courthouse to be erected in Barnet.

The Uxbridge courthouse came in the middle of this burst of activity and like Harlesden and Acton was the work of the county surveyor and architect, H T Wakelam. He adopted a free Baroque style at Uxbridge, having moved forward from the free Tudor he employed at Harlesden, but somewhat similar to his design for Acton in the same year.

The original Uxbridge courthouse, with its frontage onto Harefield Road, still stands (see p.63), but its attractive symmetry is rarely appreciated because later additions moved the main entrance to the High Street, where it begins to slope down steeply to the Frays River, making for an awkward double approach either around a corner of the building or up a long flight of steps. The site was part of the garden of a substantial house on the corner of the High Street and Harefield Road, called Hertford House (117

---

[1] *Middlesex and Buckinghamshire Advertiser, Uxbridge, Harrow and Watford Journal*, 5 Oct 1907.

[2] *Goodbye Gore* (1986), Chamberlain, Audrey (available at Harrow library).

High Street) and there were other buildings all along down the High Street to the Frays River.[3]

Harefield Road going off the High Street (c.1930). On left hand corner stands 117 High Street, part of whose garden was acquired to build Uxbridge courthouse

The main block of the former Uxbridge Union Workhouse is demolished (1967)

3 LMA: MCC/CL/L/SJ/31.

Pevsner described Wakelam's courthouse as 'a jolly building.'[4] It was built of brick with stone dressings and has some grey terracotta decoration. From the front in Harefield Road, the main three-bayed courtroom,[5] with arched windows is flanked by octagonal towers and the magistrates' and public entrances (now closed) are in gabled wings on either side. There was upstairs accommodation for a caretaker with a separate entrance on the side ('the Harefield Road car park side'). Prisoners were taken into the basement where ten cubicles for men and ten for women provided for their accommodation and there was a room each for male and female warders. Stairways communicated directly with the two courtrooms above.[6] Although there were public galleries at the back of the courtrooms, it was noted in the local newspaper that these were too small to admit more than those connected with cases being heard.

The corridor from the magistrates' entrance led to their private room.[7] At the time it commanded a splendid view over the Colne Valley into Buckinghamshire. Since then buildings have interfered with the vista, which can now only be obtained from Courtroom 3. There were rooms for the clerk to the justices on the corridor[8] leading to the magistrates' room. Waiting rooms for witnesses (male and female witnesses were kept separate), a solicitors' room and warrant officer's room were off the corridor from the public entrance and there was a central hall. It was a compact design. The builder was C F Kearley of Uxbridge and Great Marlborough Street, with a Mr F Taylor acting as local manager. An F Taylor was sitting as a magistrate in 1907, but whether or not this was the same person is unclear. The magistrates' room was heated by an open coal fire, which must have made for a pleasant focal point. The fireplace is still there, but alas empty. There was another fireplace in the clerk's room. Otherwise the whole building was heated by a low pressure hot water system and ventilated by a Boyles Air Pump in the basement. The Uxbridge & District Electric Lighting Company supplied the power for

---

4 *The Buildings of England London 3: North West* (1991), Cherry, Bridget and Pevsner, Nikolaus, Penguin Books.
5 Now Courtroom No.2.
6 Now Courtrooms Nos.1 and 2.
7 Now Retiring Room No.1.
8 Now Courtroom 2 Retiring Room and toilets.

adequate lighting. The magistrates at Wealdstone had to make do with gas lights along the front of the bench![9]

The specification set out in June 1906 stipulates how more basic needs were to be met.[10] Lavatories by Doulton were to be provided, but whilst those for the magistrates and solicitors were to have mahogany surrounds and cost £5 10s each, those for the public would cost only £2 10s. Prisoners and warders were to have extra-strong lavatories! They cost £3 10s each.

One of the rooms was set aside for the exclusive use of the Inspector of Weights and Measures and was fitted with an iron rafter to facilitate the inspection of heavy instruments. Such rooms were also installed in other new courthouses at the time.[11]

Mr H Yarrington, who had been commisionnaire at the Guildhall at Westminster, was appointed as both caretaker and usher. Police Constable Horgan was the jailer.[12]

The opening and first week of operation
The Uxbridge courthouse was opened by Sir Ralph Littler KC, chair of Middlesex Quarter Sessions, on Monday 30 September 1907. The local newspaper rose to the occasion with three columns and a photograph, at a time when the paper was not lavishly illustrated. The building was intended to be used frequently, not just for petty sessions. The chair of the bench, Mr H A Harrison, announced at the opening ceremony that the court would be open every day for indictable offences.[13] According to information on a map of boroughs and petty sessional divisions, published as part of *Bacon's Large-scale Maps of London and the Suburbs* (c.1912), the main court day at Uxbridge was Monday, but it also opened every other weekday 'if required'.[14] Arrangements had been made for the Uxbridge Urban District Council to hold its meetings in the Second Court.[15] The

---

9   *Goodbye Gore*, see earlier footnote.
10   LMA: Acc 965/5.
11   *Middlesex and Buckinghamshire Advertiser, Uxbridge, Harrow and Watford Journal*, 5 October 1907.
12   Ibid
13   Ibid
14   *The A to Z of Edwardian London* (2007), Saunders, Ann (Ed), London Topographical Society.
15   LMA: MCC/CL/SJ/4/24.

Council was to pay £50 per annum rent. The county court judge was also to be accommodated in the courthouse[16] at 10s 6d a sitting. As time went on the judge used the First Court and the county court registrar sat in the Second Court some three Tuesdays a month. The county court, which deals with civil claims, continued to use the courthouse for over 70 years.

The first magistrates' court hearings took place as soon as Sir Ralph Littler had concluded his speech and declared the courthouse open. On the Friday following the opening (4 October 1907), Mr F Taylor, sitting alone, dealt with two refractory paupers, who had refused to perform their allotted tasks whilst inmates of the casual ward at Uxbridge Union Workhouse (see the picture on p.63). The labour-master proved the case and they were each sent to prison for ten days.[17] On the Saturday, Mr Taylor again sat alone and heard George Griffin of Fulham plead guilty to being drunk at Hillingdon. He was fined five shillings. Monday October 7 saw Mr Taylor present again, but sitting with four other magistrates, Mr Tarleton being in the chair.

The local newspaper spread what must have been considered the highlights of the day across three columns.[18] A widow had left her eight-month-old twins in Royal Lane near the workhouse while she went to get a drink. Her sad story was that she had left the children in the workhouse and taken a situation in Westgate-on-Sea, which she had lost 'because she had a glass of drink'. She had returned to Uxbridge and picked up her babies, one of whom was seriously ill, before going for a drink. The policeman who found them lying on the grass took them back to 'the house' where they remained. Mr Tarleton remarked in court that he did not know what to do with the prisoner. In the event she was fined 15 shillings or 14 days and - as the money was not forthcoming - she was removed to prison. At the time the workhouse was all that stood between such tragic women and starvation, unless they were taken up by a charitable organization. Help was at hand because the Probation of Offenders Act was passed in 1907 enabling courts to make probation orders. The probation service arose out of the work of the Church of

16   LMA: MCC/C1/SJ/4/24.
17   *Middlesex and Buckinghamshire Advertiser, Uxbridge, Harrow and Watford Journal,* 12 Oct 1907.
18   Ibid.

England Temperance Society (CETS), which had been formed to rescue people who fell into crime through drunkenness.[19]

Another refractory pauper who had refused to work in the garden at the workhouse and used disgusting language to the officers there, as well as calling one of them a 'dirty tyke', was imprisoned for ten days with hard labour. He was 66 years old and had arrived at the casual ward on the Thursday and been seen by the doctor who had pronounced him fit to work. The court was told that he had been using the workhouse as a common lodging house for the past five years, usually arriving on a Saturday, when there was no medical man present, staying on Sunday when no work was done and leaving on Monday before he could be medically examined and ordered to work.

A case of wasting water brought by the district council against Frederick Wilkinson, an Uxbridge coach and motor builder was reported at length. The cistern that fed the water closet and urinal in his yard lacked a valve, causing water to run away at the rate of 80-100 gallons per hour. Magistrates found the matter proved and imposed a fine of £1 including costs. The vicar of Harmondsworth was in trouble because his dog did not have a collar with a name and address on it. He said that he knew the law, but his dog had run after a puppy and slipped his leash. Nonetheless he was fined five shillings.

Motor cars had appeared in the area and traffic offences began to enliven the court scene. Heavy fines were imposed for speeding (over 20 miles per hour). One man was fined £3 14s plus six shillings costs and another £6 14s and six shillings costs. Driving a heavy motor car without a licence warranted a fine of four shillings plus costs of ten shillings.[20] A new era had begun.

[19] www.societyguardian.co.uk And via the CETS London Police Court Mission.
[20] LMA: PS/U1/21.

CHAPTER 7

Magistrates in a New Urban World

The Metropolitan Railway reached Uxbridge from Harrow in July 1904 and offenders who had travelled on a train without paying a fare started to appear in the court (fines eight shillings with seven shillings costs or 14 days imprisonment in default of payment). The Metropolitan Line also opened up the hayfields and nursery gardens of north-west Middlesex to the possibility of development as soon as the major landowners were ready to sell their estates. Initially building was small scale and intermittent and ground to a halt during World War I, but burst out anew during the inter-war years. King's College, Cambridge and the Deanes started selling parts of their Ruislip lands in 1905; the Cox family's estates based on Hillingdon House and Harefield Place were put up for auction in 1914; Lord Hillingdon's Hillingdon Court Estate went up for sale in 1920, a year after the death of the second baron, and the Clarke-Thornhill estate in 1922. The effect upon the court was twofold. The sparsely-populated rural hinterland of Uxbridge gradually became suburban and the landed gentry who had supplied the bench with justices gradually left the district. After World War I, new commercial firms like the Bell Punch Company and Sanderson's Wallpapers opened factories at the lower end of Uxbridge on the River Colne and Grand Union Canal and the town became reasonably prosperous. The population of Elthorne was 52,830 in 1901.[1]

Changing composition of the bench

Legislative changes affected the bench. Lords lieutenants of counties had previously recommended suitable candidates to the Lord Chancellor who confirmed the appointments, which were vested in the monarch. The Liberal party swept to power in a landslide victory in 1906 and challenged this method of selecting magistrates, on the grounds that the vast majority were Conservatives. The property qualification was dropped for county magistrates, making it possible for men of smaller means to be considered and a Royal Commission on the Appointment of Justices of the Peace in

---

[1] *Victoria County History, Middlesex*, Vol 2 (1970).

1910 recommended the setting up of Advisory Committees composed of equal numbers of Liberals and Conservatives, to choose potential justices. The third Lord Hillingdon did not live in the area, but remained an Uxbridge magistrate into the 1930s.[2] After that no peer of the realm sat at Uxbridge until June 2004, when Richard Rosser, a magistrate since 1978, was created a life peer and became Lord Rosser of Ickenham. He had been General Secretary of the Transport and General Workers' Union.

In the first half of the twentieth century there was a strong link between the members of the bench and the town of Uxbridge,[3] its local government, public institutions and businesses. Justices were to be found on the Uxbridge Joint Hospital Board, the board of guardians and associated with the Old Bank, as well as sitting on the Uxbridge Urban District Council and the Middlesex County Council. Howard Stransom Button of the grocery firm Hammond Roberts and W S Try of the building firm were examples of local businessmen. Mr Button, who lived at Cedar House in Hillingdon village, is listed as an MP as well as being a magistrate in 1923.[4] The ubiquitous Charles Woodbridge, clerk to the justices, was also clerk to the Joint Hospital Board, the board of guardians, the Uxbridge Rural District Council, the county court and to the Commissioners of Inland Revenue. He was also superintendent registrar and his nephew Algernon Rivers Woodbridge was his deputy in that role. Francis Charles Woodbridge of the same family and firm of solicitors was clerk to Uxbridge United Charities. Henry William Woodbridge, another relative was on the bench[5]. The various Uxbridge charities had been united in 1907 and the following year new almshouses, built off New Windsor Street, were named Woodbridge House to commemorate the family's long service to the charities.[6]

Uxbridge became an urban district in 1894 and achieved borough status in 1955. Mayors of boroughs and chairmen of district councils sat on local benches *ex officio* during their terms of office and some remained on the bench afterwards. Over the years a number of councillors and

2 *Kelly's Directory* (1933).
3 *King's and Kelly's Directories* (1900-1950).
4 *King's 'Gazette' Directory* (1923).
5 *Kelly's Directory* (1910).
6 *Uxbridge: A Concise History* (1982), Hearmon Carolynne, p.72.

aldermen, from the urban district councils in the area[7] have sat at Uxbridge. A newcomer in the early 1970s had the impression that 'there were a lot of councillors and aldermen on the bench and a lot of Rotarians!'

Women

Meanwhile women had made strides in education, being able to take degrees at the University of London and some other places, but not yet at Oxford or Cambridge. Movements like the Women's Cooperative Guild (founded in 1883) were raising the consciousness of working-class women to their needs and giving them the self-confidence to give witness to the shortcomings of the social system. There was a growing realisation that women needed power at the ballot box to change legislation to achieve welfare reform and equality with men in such matters as divorce settlements and custody of children.

The Suffragettes were becoming increasingly frustrated by the constant rejection of their reasoned petitions for the right to vote. Eventually, after World War I, Parliament accepted the major contribution made by women to the war effort and extended the franchise to a limited number of women, (those who were married and over 30) and introduced the Sex Disqualification Removal Act in 1919. Within days Ada Summers, the wealthy widow of an ironmaster, active suffragist and Mayor of Staleybridge, was sworn in as a JP. As mayor she had a right to sit on the bench, but Mrs Summers had been disqualified by her sex. In the next five years 1,200 women were appointed across England and Wales as JPs overall and thereafter about 100 each year. Many of the early women justices, e.g. Beatrice Webb, were active in revealing social injustice generally and promoting advances for women in public life.

Two of the four women who sat on the Uxbridge bench before the World War II were as active politically as any of their male colleagues. Flora Mary Baker of Danemead, Northolt, joined the Uxbridge bench in 1922 and sat until 1948. She had represented Northolt on Uxbridge Rural District Council from 1919 and on Ealing Council from 1928 after the abolition of the Uxbridge RDC. She was elected to Middlesex County

---

[7] Hayes and Harlington, Ruislip-Northwood, Uxbridge, Yiewsley and West Drayton - and, after 1964, the London Borough of Hillingdon.

Council in 1931 and became an alderman in 1948.[8] Mrs Baker was soon joined by Mrs D Law of Dawley Lodge in 1924 and Miss Angela Mary Wakefield of New Belmont in 1929, both of whom were related to male magistrates. Mrs Kathleen Lovibond, widow of an Uxbridge solicitor, joined the bench in 1934.[9]

The mundane problem of providing a 'lady magistrates' lavatory' was dealt with expeditiously and cheaply. The clerks were to use the magistrates' facilities, leaving their own to be adapted by putting a 'Ladies only' sign on the door and installing a looking glass.[10]

Mrs Lovibond opening Yiewsley Conservative Fete in July 1935

Kathleen Lovibond first came to Uxbridge because she had joined the Women's Auxiliary Air Corps in 1917. She married William Oliver Lovibond in 1924, had two children and was elected to the Middlesex County Council in 1928 to represent Uxbridge. Pneumonia killed her husband and daughter within days of each other in 1929, but she continued her life of public service. She was chair of the MCC Maternity and Child Welfare Committee and the Public Assistance Committee and

---

[8] Ealing Library: index *Middlesex County Times*: information from Jonathan Oates, local history librarian.

[9] King's *'Gazette' Directory* (1924; 1929).

[10] LMA: MCC/CL/SJ/4/26.

was later appointed alderman. She resigned from the MCC in 1945 to concentrate on the juvenile court of which she became chair in 1947. She was invited to serve on Sir John Wolfenden's committee inquiring into the laws relating to homosexual offences and prostitution in 1954 and received a CBE for public service in 1955. When the political parties on the council of the new Borough of Uxbridge found themselves equally balanced in 1956, they invited Mrs Lovibond, as a public figure who was not a councillor, to become mayor. She left Uxbridge and the bench in 1959 after she married a Mr Squibb, and moved out of the area. She died in 1976 aged 82.[11] During her time on the bench she twice benefited from a quaint custom whereby the clerk presented a pair of white gloves to a magistrate if he or she were not required to sit through lack of business.[12]

Shortly before the outbreak of the Second World War, there were still just three women on the bench out of a total membership of 32.[13] Following a Royal Commission on Justices of the Peace in 1947, the Magistrates' Association (founded 1920) recommended immediate steps to increase the number of women on each bench. Figures are not available to show how quickly women infiltrated the ranks at Uxbridge, but justices appointed as recently as 1972 had the impression that there were far fewer women than men. The *Middlesex Area Magistrates' Committee Year Book* for 1982-3 shows 64 male and 34 female magistrates. In 1987 the Uxbridge bench increased in size because the Gore division had been abolished and divided between Brent and Harrow in the shake up following the abolition of the Greater London Council. All sitting magistrates were invited to move benches if they wished and some moved to Uxbridge, bringing the total to 120 (70 men and 50 women). The *Justices Year Book 2007* shows near parity between the sexes on the Uxbridge Bench - with 55 men and 53 women - but it had taken a long time to achieve.

Although women have played an active part in bench affairs, with many serving as deputies, there have been only three female chairmen of the Uxbridge bench. Blanche Brierley who was a journalist was the earliest, from 1976-78. She had given up her career upon marriage, but was president of the National Council of Women. Lavinia Cox of Roundwood House, Harefield, who had worked as a production engineer in an aircraft

---

[11] Pearce, Ken, 'A Life of Public Service', *Uxbridge Record*, No. 28 and 29.

[12] Orton, Leslie, *Half a Century at Uxbridge*, Report (1989).

[13] *Kelly's Directory* (1938).

factory during the war before going to the Overseas Finance Division of the Treasury, became a JP in 1963 and was chairman of the bench in 1980.[14] She was also organizer of the Citizens' Advice Bureau in Yiewsley and a member of the Council of Brunel University, founded in Uxbridge in 1966. Margaret Bunford, one of the 1972 bench intake, served two consecutive terms from 1988-93 and was particularly interested in the work of the probation liaison committee (PLC). Her background was in social work.

Although women still wore hats on the Uxbridge bench until 1965-6, they were not just 'ladies who lunched'. Several ran businesses. One woman, long remembered for the strong-arm methods she used to extract fines from offenders, had her own successful hat shop in Ealing. Others were in teaching, in schools and higher education, often being a head of department. The nursing and legal professions were also represented. There were a number of women attached to the local council and the Cooperative movement. A large number of the women came onto the bench with great administrative ability and public speaking skills, honed in voluntary work for various charitable organizations.

During the 1980s and 1990s a group of Uxbridge magistrates became associated with the work of HM Prison Service as prison visitors at Feltham Young Offender Institution. This was separate from their bench work and came about because Norman Mulliner was chairman of the board of visitors[15] (1983-90) and encouraged colleagues to take an interest.

The Probation Service[16]

In the same year that the courthouse opened, the Probation of Offenders Act 1907 made it possible for courts to appoint probation officers, to release first offenders on probation and make probation orders. Courts were not required to have probation officers until 1925. Since 1876 workers from the Church of England Temperance Society (CETS) had been attached to some police courts (as they were usually then known) as 'court missionaries'. This direct connection between the probation service and the Church of England was not severed until 1936. Probation officers' duties were 'to advise, assist and befriend' probationers and there was a call for formal training for them in 1919. They have played an enormous and

---

[14] *Magistrates of Harefield*, Jarvis, Donald (available from Uxbridge Library).
[15] Now the Independent Monitoring Board (IMB).
[16] Now the National Probation Service (NPS) under the Ministry of Justice.

impressive role in the rehabilitation of offenders and prevention of recidivism over the years, despite changing attitudes, ideas and regimes. Uxbridge made use of the 1907 Act almost immediately. On 11 February 1908 two boys aged 14 and 15 who had been found sleeping in a field without visible means of subsistence were 'bound over under the Probation of Offenders Act 1907.'[17] At Uxbridge, early probation officers had to share the clerk's room and probationers waiting to be interviewed had to stand in the corridor.

Children's courts

The Childrens Act 1908 - known as the 'Children's Charter' - brought separate children's courts into being, but there was no special training for magistrates dealing with children until after the passing of the Children and Young Persons Act of 1933. Magistrates were then elected by their colleagues in each petty sessional division to sit in the juvenile court. At Uxbridge the 'children's court' sat once a month in the early years, using the magistrates' room. Those waiting to be seen had to wait in the corridor.

The Juvenile Register for 1933-40 shows boys of 16 being fined half a crown for lighting fireworks in the street, and a group of five boys aged between nine and 14 who were gathered together in a warehouse in Coldharbour Lane for unlawful purposes being discharged with a caution.[18] There were several bind-overs and occasionally parents were fined for their children's misdemeanours. A 14-year-old boy 'beyond control' was placed on probation for two years and a 16-year-old was sent to Rowley Hall, an approved school at Stafford, for two years. A boy of 15, found guilty of larceny was placed in 'the care of a fit person', in this case Dr. W Max Wilson of Ruislip, until he was 17. When women joined the bench, some naturally sat in the juvenile court and several have chaired it at Uxbridge. One retired magistrate who began her career in 1961 on an Essex bench, was asked to become a magistrate because of a rape case involving a juvenile, when it was thought essential to have a woman present. The 'juvenile bench' was renamed 'youth court' in 1992 and the 'juvenile panel' the 'youth court panel'.

---

[17] LMA/PS/U1/20.
[18] LMA: PS/U4/1.

Extra business and increased costs

Charles Woodbridge (1830-1924) weathered many changes during his long period as clerk to the justices from 1874 until his death, still in harness, at the age of 94. He lived at Heath Lodge on Park Road and his salary for the part-time job was £350 per annum around the time that the new courthouse was built. New legislation dealing with motor cars, children and probation brought additional duties for the clerk, as did such things as claims by members of the public for exemption from dog licence duty. He applied to the SJC for an increase in salary on those grounds early in 1914 and was awarded £400 'for all business which he may by reason of his office be called upon to perform.'[19] Among the bundle of correspondence there is a questionnaire, which he filled in, giving information about the court and showing a high proportion of time spent on dispensing summary justice. During the year ending 30 June 1913 there had been:

- 414 fresh charges and 48 adjourned charges;
- 564 summonses;
- 138 rate summonses and 44 adjourned summonses;
- eight cases committed for trial at Assizes or Quarter Sessions;
- 200 licensed premises and 83 related licensing applications; and
- similarly with regard to 13 registered clubs.

The number of sittings was between 13 and 14 per month. These normally began at eleven o'clock in the morning and continued 'to the time when business ends'. The number of sittings per year, including special sessions and occasional courts, was 161. The First Court sat on 161 days; the Second Court on 22 days; and the children's court eleven days. One clerk's whole time was occupied by court work on days when the court was not sitting. The clerk to the justices provided clerical assistance, stationery etc.

Charles Woodbridge was in private practice at 38 High Street, Uxbridge in the long-established solicitor's firm of Messrs Woodbridge and Sons, and the out-of-court administrative work was done from his place of business by one of his own employees. Not until 1939 were court staff employed, accommodated and paid directly by the Middlesex SJC rather than the clerk to the justices. He was probably well-worth £400 a year as he was effectively running the court for that sum. Also his office in

---

[19] LMA: MCC/CL/L/SJ/12.

the courthouse was available for use by probation officers and others on the days when courts were not sitting.

Uxbridge Court House showing 1970s frontage

The modern-day view from Harefield Road

CHAPTER 8

Meeting the Demands of Increasing Business

Some justices of the peace came to court by car and as traffic increased the police began clearing parked vehicles from Harefield Road. The layout at the front of the courthouse was altered in 1927 to provide 'a draw-up' for cars and in 1930 the land on the north side of the courthouse was acquired for a car park.[1] An extra piece of land adjoining the car park was bought a few years later and is the area where the prison vans now draw up.

The Probation Committee[2] protested about their unsuitable accommodation in 1932 and the Standing Joint Committee (SJC) agreed that up to £1,000 could be spent on a single storey extension where a new room would be provided for the inspector of weights and measures, leaving the inspector's old room free for probation officers. A new office was to be provided for the warrant officer, who had been working for some time from the basement near the holding cells and boiler. W S Try, the Uxbridge builder, put in an acceptable tender of £970 and the new offices were completed in 1934.[3] They were at the south-west corner of the building. Further refurbishments were made, mainly new furniture and decorations in 1938 to provide for the clerk's staff. They were still located at Charles Woodbridge's premises until they moved in November 1938, leaving behind old deposition books and papers, cluttering up the Woodbridge and Sons storeroom, leading to threats that the documents would be destroyed unless taken to the courthouse.[4] The SJC ordered their immediate transfer.

By the time that Laurance H Crossley became clerk to the justices in 1946 (*Chapter 5*), the courthouse was inadequate. In his own short history of the courthouse, he describes an atmosphere of gloom and depression in both courtrooms, with benches and forms in the well of the courts which had come from the Educational Supply Association (and that did not

---

[1] LMA: MCC/CL/SJ/4/26.
[2] A county committee preceding Probation Boards/the National Probation Service (NPS).
[3] LMA: MCC/CL/SJ/4/26.
[4] Ibid.

comply with the specifications of 1906).[5] The space in the courthouse was being used even more than it had been before World War II. The coroner used the First Court on Fridays. There was by then a domestic court[6] on Wednesdays (to deal with matrimonial and similar cases) as well as the then juvenile court on Fridays, each held in the magistrates' room.

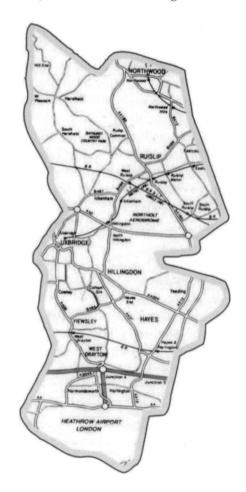

Proximity to Heathrow Airport ensures interesting business

---

[5] *The Uxbridge Court House 1907-1982* (1982), Crossley, Laurance H (unpublished). Made available by Veronica Clifford of Uxbridge Magistrates' Court.

[6] Now the family proceedings court.

An extension was built in 1953, the year of the coronation of Queen Elizabeth II. A wing was added to the south side of the main building, leading down the Harefield Road frontage. The land on which it was built (another part of the garden of 117 High Street) had been acquired by compulsory purchase order in 1935.[7] There was a large room for either the domestic court or juvenile court and two waiting rooms, one for those awaiting the hearing of a contested case and a separate one for those who had already given evidence or been dealt with and who were ready either to go home, or to be taken into custody. This 'one-way system' prevented discussions between the two groups. There was also a general office and an office for the clerk to the justices in the new wing. The opening ceremony was performed by Dr Gerald Ellison, Bishop of Willesden.

An interesting feature of the new juvenile/domestic courtroom was a mobile witness stand on wheels. On one occasion a policeman in a hurry stepped onto it with too much force and found himself shooting across the room to general amusement.[8]

Heathrow Airport gradually expanded and had become a major airport with millions of passengers by 1963, bringing much business to Uxbridge Magistrates' Court, some – e.g. major smuggling cases or 'drug swallowers' – adding to the breadth and interest of magistrates' work. Most of the increased workload was less inspiring, being concerned with motoring (traffic in the area around the airport had increased), taxi-touts and dishonest baggage handlers. Laurance Crossley noted that constant contact between the same offenders and the same police officers caused

> a degree of bitterness on both sides, ultimately wasting court time with cases being fought to the bitter end, which could probably have been avoided if sweet reasonableness had generally prevailed.[9]

With all this extra work it was time, in 1963, for another extension, this time upwards. A third court (now Courtroom No.3) was built above the Second Court (now Courtroom 1) and probation offices were added above the juvenile/domestic court and general office. The ground floor was extended at the same time, making another new office for the clerk to the

---

[7] LMA: MCC/CL/SJ/4/26.

[8] *Half a Century at Uxbridge*, Orton, Leslie, Uxbridge Magistrates' Report for 1989.

[9] *The Uxbridge Court House 1907-1982* (see footnote 5).

justices. During the alterations, use was made of the Congregational Church Hall in Beasleys Yard, for road traffic and domestic courts. According to Laurance Crossley the biblical texts around the walls, relating to peace and love did not accord well with the regular slanging matches between husbands and wives in court! The Women's Royal Voluntary Service (WRVS) began to supply light refreshments from a very small cubby-hole under the new stairs leading from the public entrance hall.

The WRVS provided much needed refreshment to court users

The 75-year-old Middlesex County Council was abolished and the Greater London Council (GLC), divided into boroughs, was established in 1964. The county itself, first recorded in 707, was also officially lost. The Uxbridge bench was situated in the new Borough of Hillingdon. The five London Commission Areas for the Administration of Justice were given purely geographical names and the Uxbridge area was to have become London North West, but after a fight supported by Sir Christopher Cowan of Kiln Farm, Northwood, former chairman of the Middlesex County Council and chairman of the Uxbridge bench 1947-64, it was named the Middlesex Area, keeping some connection with its Saxon roots. It was administered by the Middlesex Area Magistrates' Courts Committee from the Guildhall in Westminster.

By 1973 further offices and courtrooms were needed at the courthouse and a new home was desperately needed for the county court which occupied Courtroom 1 for a whole day each week. The GLC architect designed the extension, which was built between 1976-9. A new building for the county court and a tax office were built on the land next to the court house about the same time. The land occupied by Nos. 114-116 High Street along the High Street frontage was acquired in 1972 and the proposals were approved by the GLC and Home Office in 1974.[10] Cherry and Pevsner described the buildings as 'the unsatisfactory Court House and Inland Revenue Offices, bitty 1970s affairs in red brick, just where a solid street front is needed to lead the eye downwards.'[11]

Notwithstanding any visual shortcomings, the new extension to the courthouse provided two new courtrooms (Courtroom No.4 and Courtroom No. 5), a new entrance foyer and a new two-storey probation building, with an underground car-park beneath. Although the extension sits rather unhappily with the original 1907 courthouse, it blends better with the 1953 wing, and certainly provides most of the facilities needed in a modern courthouse, although there is a common entrance for all court users (except those in custody) and there are probably other security issues in the modern age. The cost was £1,300,000.

When Lord Hailsham performed the opening ceremony in May 1979, making his first appearance as Lord Chancellor in the new Conservative Government, he was horrified to find that there was often a delay of several months before cases came to trial. 'A wait of three or four weeks is tolerable and more is unacceptable'[12] he said. He inspected the graffiti in the cells, saying, 'There is nothing new here. Still little imagination', but when he saw it in rooms where child offenders were taken he said sharply, 'That should be wiped off'. He also commented tartly on the large number of steps, 'What if you have a disabled magistrate?' The new building was blessed by the Bishop of Kensington, the Rt. Reverend Ronald Goodchild.

Uxbridge courthouse now had five courtrooms and each of the 50 or so establishment of magistrates had to sit more frequently than the Lord Chancellor preferred. He believed that they would become too

---

[10] Uxbridge Magistrates' Court Opening Ceremony: Veronica Clifford.
[11] *The Buildings of England London 3 North West* (1991), Cherry B and Pevsner N.
[12] Uxbridge Library: Cuttings Book, p.286, *Hillingdon Mirror*.

'professional'. The number had increased to 98 by the time that Laurance Crossley, having overseen the changes to the courthouse, retired in 1982.

The GLC did not last long and on 1 April 1986 the Uxbridge bench found itself in the Hillingdon Petty Sessional Area[13] within the Middlesex Commission Area and was run by the Middlesex Area Magistrates' Courts Committee. The Middlesex Commission Area comprised Barnet, Brent, Ealing, Enfield, Haringey, Harrow, Hillingdon and Hounslow. At the same time there was a change in the way cases were prosecuted. This had previously been done by the police, but now the Crown Prosecution Service (CPS) was established. Crown prosecutors first appeared at Uxbridge in October 1986 following the Prosecution of Offences Act 1985.

Middlesex petty sessional areas

The training of magistrates

The introduction of specialised courts and the intervention of probation officers meant that justices needed a greater understanding of offenders,

---

[13] Petty sessional areas (PSAs) were formerly known as petty sessional divisions (PSDs) and are now known as 'local justice areas'.

their motives, the range of sentences available and their likely effect. The need for training became more apparent after the Criminal Justice Act, 1948, and the Justices of the Peace Act 1949 introduced more changes. A Magistrates' Court Committee (MCC) was established in each area in 1953, responsible for administering the court and providing training for magistrates. There may have been some reluctance on the part of long-serving magistrates to 'go back to school', so in 1966 training became compulsory for all new magistrates.

𝔐𝔦𝔡𝔡𝔩𝔢𝔰𝔢𝔵 𝔔𝔲𝔞𝔯𝔱𝔢𝔯 𝔖𝔢𝔰𝔰𝔦𝔬𝔫𝔰 𝔄𝔯𝔢𝔞

of 𝔊𝔯𝔢𝔞𝔱𝔢𝔯 𝔏𝔬𝔫𝔡𝔬𝔫

EPIPHANY QUARTER SESSION
JANUARY 1967

Rota of Justices until the day of the Epiphany Quarter Session, 1968, who will be prepared to accompany the Troops in case of Riots or apprehended Riots within the County.

(1 GEO. 1, STATUTE 2, CAP. 5.)

Name of Justice.	Address.	Petty Sessional Division.	Name of Justice.	Address.	Petty Sessional Division.	Name of Justice.
mstrong, Esq.	101, Arundel Drive, Boreham Wood, Herts.	(Edmonton and Tottenham District)	G. A. Davies, Esq.	"Strathaven," 33, Beech Hill, Hadley Wood, Barnet, Herts.	NEW SPELTHORNE	R. Crimble, Esq. ... T
Boyle, Esq.	Wood House, Hadley Common, Barnet, Herts.					R. H. Gibbs, Esq. ... "
			A. C. Goddard, Esq., F.C.A.	26, Windhill, Bishop's Stortford, Herts.		S. H. Hyde, Esq. ... K
F. Reynolds, Esq.	38, West Hill Way, Totteridge, N.20.		A. H. Roullier, Esq.	278, Croyland Road, Edmonton, N.8.		Lt.-Col. P. A. Symmons, M.C., D.L. L
Ritchie, Esq., L.D.S., S.	107, Sandpit Lane, St. Albans, Herts.		J. B. Turner, Esq.	39, The Birches, Winchmore Hill, N.21.		
		(Wood Green District)	S. Dawson, Esq., M.I.E.E.	60, Hounsden Road, Winchmore Hill, N.21.	UXBRIDGE	L. Lambert, Esq. ... I!
Denton, Esq., D.L., I.S.	30, Osterley Road, Isleworth.		A. L. Everett, Esq., F.R.I.C.S.	"Wildwoods," Theobalds Park Road, Enfield, Middlesex.		N. J. H. Neale, Esq. ... I'
V. E. F. Elborne	14, Chancellor House, Hyde Park Gate, S.W.7.		J. B. Turner, Esq.	39, The Birches, Winchmore Hill, N.21.		R. J. Page, Esq., A.M.I.H.E. G
Marks, Esq.	The Swan Inn, Swan Street, Isleworth.		Mrs. R. Winston-Fox, B.Sc.	4, Morton Crescent, Southgate, N.14.		W. L. Try, Esq. ... M
Rockman, Esq., .K., D.L.	36, Leigh Gardens, Kensal Rise, N.W.10.	GORE				

Justices who would be prepared to accompany troops in the case of riots 1967

One member of the bench who joined the Uxbridge court in 1968 remembers receiving a letter from Guildhall telling him that he must do his fair share of work at petty sessions and at Quarter Sessions. He then received a letter from Laurance Crossley inviting him to visit the court at his convenience 'to observe.' For some time he attended court and sat on the bench as a dummy, until Mr Crossley deemed that the time was right to give him some instruction and put him on the rota. Laurance Crossley undertook all the original teaching in Uxbridge, drawing on his wealth of experience.

The Judicial Studies Board (JSB) was set up in 1979 and participation in continuous training became expected of all justices. At Uxbridge, David

Simpson, clerk to the justices (1982-92), his successor Martin Hamilton (1992-2003) and Judith Nichols, head of legal services, organized it. Probation officers working with the probation liaison committee (PLC) provided training based on the courses being introduced for various types of offenders. In the late-1980s, new magistrates received three days of formal training before being added to the rota. This was followed about a year later with a weekend at Ashridge and visits to penal institutions and the various customs suites at Heathrow Airport. They also attended 'continuing training' along with more experienced magistrates.

The Magistrates' Association played an important role in organizing training conferences and courses. A system based on skills, competences and appraisals came in 1998 with the introduction of the Magistrates' National Training Initiative (MNTI). This was refined by 'MNTI 2' in 2004-2005. Mentors are appointed for new magistrates. One aim has been to enhance decision-making and help magistrates to reach structured decisions, especially important since one consequence of the Human Rights Act 1998 is that they must announce and record reasons for their findings. Bench books, which set out clear guidelines on sentencing, have been given to all magistrates since 2004.

Retirement

Justices used to stay in office until death or ill health prevented them from attending court. The Justices of the Peace Act 1968 reduced the retiring age gradually from 75 to 70, where it remains. The 1968 Act also first defined the relationship between legal advisers and JPs, the former being confirmed as having a duty to tender advice on law and other aspects of justices' powers; the latter solely responsible making findings of fact and, e.g. concerning the credibility of witnesses. Magistrates also decide the appropriate sentence subject now to the work of the Sentencing Guidelines Council (SGC) and advice on any legal implications from the clerk.

The Crown Court

Local justices continued to attend Quarter Sessions at the Middlesex Guildhall in Westminster until 1971 when the Courts Act of that year abolished both the old Assize Courts and Quarter Sessions, replacing them with the Crown Court. Uxbridge justices who went to Quarter Sessions remember that some judges were welcoming and cooperative, whilst others seemed to regard the magistrates as a nuisance. After Middlesex Guildhall became a Crown Court centre, Uxbridge magistrates continued to visit and sit there until an old people's home at Isleworth was converted into a more locally-based Crown Court in the 1970s. Sometimes justices sat with the judge on jury trials, but only as observers. They had no input, but there were training benefits to be derived from watching and listening to the judge. One magistrate remembers being invited into the retiring room with a judge who was sentencing a convicted prisoner. The judge explained why he thought that a deferred sentence was appropriate, but did not ask for an opinion from the magistrate. Uxbridge magistrates sat on licensing appeals at the Crown Court, also in the 1970s, and occasionally went to Southwark Crown Court. Now local magistrates, after two years on the bench and a training visit, sit with judges at the Crown Court at Isleworth on appeals, and sentencing in reports cases as well. Their opinion is always sought by the judge.

Middlesex Guildhall ceased to be a Crown Court centre in April 2007, when it closed in preparation for its transformation into the Supreme Court of the United Kingdom, due to open in 2009.

The family bench

The family proceedings court was instituted in October 1991 following the passing of the Childrens Act 1989. It replaced the domestic court.[14] Fairly soon, family cases began occupying several days a week and could not occupy Court 5, its usual venue, for such long periods without disrupting other court business. The former caretaker's quarters on the first floor were refurbished and became the Elthorne Suite in 1993.[15] The suite is used for meetings and training as well as family courts. When the Greater London Magistrates' Courts Authority (GLMCA) was established in April 2001, threats to amalgamate family courts and establish family centres in three parts of London, all distant from Uxbridge, caused alarm to members of the Uxbridge family bench, knowing the difficulty of getting clients who usually have young or school age children, even to the local court in time. The Uxbridge family court has survived so far and extra accommodation

---

[14] Sometimes called the 'matrimonial court', but it also dealt, e.g. with affiliation (formerly known as 'bastardy') cases.

[15] It is good to see the Saxon name for the division of Middlesex in which the court is situated, revived in this way.

was made available for some cases to be heard at the Uxbridge county court premises, situated in Hayes, in 2006.

The modern-day magistrates' court

Much concern arose latter in the twentieth century over the general perception that magistrates were 'middle-aged, middle-class and middle-minded', and not representative of the population as a whole. Having achieved near parity between the sexes on the bench, recruitment of members of ethnic minority groups, became an issue. The 2001 census shows that the population of the borough of Hillingdon was 243,006 with an ethnic minority of 20.4 per cent.[16] In fact there had been members of ethnic minorities, especially Jews, on the bench for many years, but not specially noted as such, except in Brent where it had sometimes been difficult to find a bench on Fridays! By 1988 there were three men from minority groups at Uxbridge and the number had risen to 17, including six women by 2007.

A feature in the local newspaper, *The Gazette* (21 July 1999) demonstrated the diversity of newly-appointed magistrates, so far as social class, sex and ethnicity went. One woman worked at the Inland Revenue office, another was a retired teacher; of the three men, one was a 'bus driver and an officer of the Trades and General Workers' Union', another was a regional manager for Guinness, the brewers, and the third was a customs officer. One man and one woman represented ethnic minorities. *The Gazette* article explained that magistrates were supposed to be representative of their community, of varying ages, with different points of view and come from different backgrounds. Although that newspaper did not mention it, all justices are united by their oaths or affirmations of allegiance and judicial office:

I swear by Almighty God that I will be faithful to Her Majesty, Queen Elizabeth II, Her heirs and successors according to law. **Oath of Allegiance**

I swear by Almighty God that I will well and truly serve our Sovereign Lady, Queen Elizabeth the Second, in the office of Justice of the Peace, and I will do right to all manner of people after the laws and usages of this realm without fear or favour, affection or ill will. **The Judicial Oath**

---

[16] Uxbridge Library: Population figures.

A feature of the court since the 1980s has been the presence on the bench of the Holy books of the major religions to enable everyone taking the oath to do so according to their religious principles.

Further efforts to reach the wider community and help to impart a better understanding of the work done by magistrates were made in the 1990s at the instigation of the Magistrates' Association. Magistrates made contact with local senior schools, gave talks and sat in the public gallery with groups that visited the court house, explaining the court procedures and answering questions. In 1995, an initiative named 'Magistrates into the Community' was set up to widen the scope of the project to clubs, local societies and all kinds of community groups. Presentations in primary schools have proved popular with both teachers and children.

The proximity of airports has brought at least one visit from a foreign dignitary to the court. The French minister of justice with his entourage flew into Heathrow one morning in February 1994 to see how our legal system worked with lay justices. He came into a family court (with special permission because the public are not normally admitted) and asked Martin Hamilton, who was conducting him around the court, what the three magistrates did in ordinary life. One was retired, one taught history and the other organized musical concerts for charity. It all sounded rather more splendid translated into French! The French party was then whisked away, apparently impressed by the time and care given by lay magistrates to their cases. The chair of the bench and clerk to the justices enjoyed dinner at the French Embassy that evening.

'Centre of Excellence'

Uxbridge Court was awarded the 'Centre of Excellence' award in 1997, because of its 'excellent management, with a happy, well-informed and well-motivated staff, committed to and delivering a very high quality of service.'[17] Martin Hamilton, clerk to the justices was 'thrilled'. The court staff had been increasing throughout the twentieth century. In 1997 there were 48 full-time and five part-time staff including clerks and ushers, all supporting 127 magistrates.[18]

As already indicated, the lay magistrates, who are unpaid, run their own hearings, but could not do so without the support of the court staff.

---

[17] Uxbridge Library: Cuttings Book
[18] 'Aiming to be a Centre of Excellence', Uxbridge Magistrates' Court.

The well-trained and friendly clerks, always ready with appropriate judicial advice, ensure the legal probity of the magistrates. The staff who are most familiar to justices are those who man the front desk and the ever good-humoured and unflappable ushers, who strive to keep the courts moving and preserve peace in the waiting rooms with calm politeness. The court produces an immense amount of paper work each day, dealt with by competent, but perhaps under strength office staff. Mainly unseen, there are officers down below in the cells who take care of the prisoners. Nowadays at Uxbridge, the whole of this is managed by an excellent bench office manager. So far as the justices are concerned, however, Veronica Clifford, justices' liaison officer and rota coordinator is the pivot around which the court revolves.

The centralisation of courts in the greater London area under the GLMCA that came into being on 1 April 2001 meant a loss of autonomy and Uxbridge and other courts entered a rather unsettled period. The GLMCA was replaced by Her Majesty's Court Service in April 2005, now, since March 2007, part of a new Ministry of Justice (MOJ) (alongside prisons, probation and parole which passed to the MOJ from the Home Office at the same time). The change brought about an amalgamation of Hendon, Barnet, Brent, Harrow and Uxbridge under one justices' clerk, Gaynor Houghton-Jones. Plans are now being discussed in detail for 'clustering' courts to make better services available from large centres well-provided with resources. It looks as if Uxbridge Magistrates' Court is all set to continue to dispense local justice for the foreseeable future. We must wish it luck in the next hundred years ... or so.

Chairmen of the Uxbridge Bench: Norman Mulliner, Blanch Brierley, David Simpson, clerk to the justices, Margaret Bunford, Derek Blackwell and Eric Wise.

Staff and magistrates in party mood: Reza Ali (formerly a court clerk and now a local solicitor), Kay Buxton JP, Ann Sibley (fines department), Peter Rogers JP and Brenda Paul (then responsible for licensing and now in the listing department)

Appendix

Chairmen of the Uxbridge Bench 1855-2007

1855-65 Thomas Dagnall III of Cowley Place, Cowley. Member of a corn milling family. JP 1831.

1865-85 Thomas Truesdale Clarke 1802-90, of Swakeleys, Ickenham.

1885-92 Francis Henry Deane 1814-92, of Eastcote House, Ruislip.

1892-97 Lt. Colonel Arthur Charles Greville 1827-1901, of The Chestnuts, Hillingdon. Associated with Uxbridge Old Bank.

1897-1904 Robert Edward Master b.1826, of Hillingdon Furze, Hillingdon. JP 1883.

1904-1919 *No record.*

1919-21 A H Tarleton 1862-1921, of Breakspears, Harefield. Royal Navy (Active List) 1874-88; Commander on Emergency List 1913. JP 1891-1921.

1921-31 Cecil Fane de Salis 1857-1948, of Dawley Court. JP 1895-1938.

1931-33 Walter S Glynn. JP 1919-33.

1933-47 Sir Gilfrid Craig DL. JP 1922.

1947-64 Sir Christopher Cowan 1889-1979. JP 1949.

1964-67 Dr. Kenneth MacFarlane. JP 1937.

1968-71 Leonard Lambert FCIS. JP 1956.

1972-75 William John Lipscombe. JP 1950.

1976-78	Blanche M Brierley. JP 1951.
1979	W Darrell Charles. JP 1955.
1980-83	Lavinia Cox. JP 1963.
1984	Eric F Wise. JP 1967.
1985-87	Norman Mulliner.
1987-92	Margaret Bunford. JP 1972.
1993-95	Derek Blackwell. JP 1973.
1996-2000	Richard Rosser. JP 1978.
2001-03	Derek Stobbs. JP 1988.
2003 –	Richard Bristow. JP 1985.

Index